Daily Meditations
(with Scripture)
for Busy Couples

David Fortier and Patricia Robertson

ACTA Publications

Chicago, Illinois

Daily Meditations (with Scripture)
for Busy Couples
by David Fortier and Patricia Robertson

David Fortier is the publisher and editor of *The American Catholic* in Bristol, Connecticut, and the author of numerous essays and articles in a variety of secular and religious publications. Patricia Robertson is the pastoral coordinator at St. Catherine Laboure Catholic Church in Concord, Michigan, and the author of *Daily Meditations (with Scripture) for Busy Moms*.

Edited by Gregory F. Augustine Pierce
Cover art by Abigail Pierce (age 4) and Isz
Design and Typesetting by Garrison Publications

Published by ACTA Publications, 4848 N. Clark St. Chicago, IL 60640 (773) 271-1030

Library of Congress Catalog Number: 96-80170

ISBN: 0-87946-156-X

Printed in the United States of America

01 00 99 98 97 5 4 3 2 1 First Printing

Happy Anniversary

Happy Anniversary, sweetheart. Was it really so many years ago we wed, on a New Year's Day not unlike today?

Happy Anniversary, dear. With each new year we made a new beginning, pledged our love again.

Happy New Year, honey. I love you more now than I ever could have imagined on that first New Year's Day.

Happy New Year, lover. Will you marry me again?

So if anyone is in Christ, there is a new creation: everything old has passed away; see, everything has become new.
                    2 Corinthians 5:17

Cold feet on mine in the middle of the night. Then warm caresses, tender touch. We both awake and hold each other.

You chase away my nightmares, the demons that haunt my sleep. Inside you, I am comforted and reassured.

Please, make love to me.

Then she came stealthily and uncovered his feet, and lay down. At midnight the man was startled, and turned over, and there, lying at his feet, was a woman!

Ruth 3:7-8

You Call First

Should I call her?

I don't want her to think
I've given in.

Still, I want her to know I
still love her.

Maybe I should swallow
my pride.

I never want to hurt her.

Should I call her?

Should I call him?

I don't want him to think
I've given in.

Still, I want him to know I
still love him.

Maybe I should swallow
my pride.

I never want to hurt him.

Should I call him?

---

*Even if you draw your sword against a
friend, do not despair, for there is a way
back. If you open your mouh against your
friend, do not worry, for re onciliation is
possible.*

Sirach 22:21-22

Impasse

I'm no sentimentalist, but I still look forward to our getting out alone together. Between our busy schedules, however, we haven't done anything special for a while.

I want to talk about it, and I don't want to talk about it.

Impasse.

All the people shouted and said, "Great is truth and strongest of all!" Then the king said to him, "Ask what you wish, even beyond what is written, and we will give it to you."

1 Esdras 4:41-42

> *Soul Mates*

You're out of town—on business, or taking care of a relative, or on a much-deserved vacation or retreat by yourself.

I hunger for you. I am somehow closer to you now than when I let our daily routine numb me to your presence, your body, your essence.

We may be apart, but we aren't separated.

We are joined at the soul. We are soul mates.

———————————

Now the whole group of those who believed were of one heart and soul.

Acts 4:32

The Mysterious World of Men

"You just don't get it," he says.

He's right. I don't get it. I don't know what it's like to be a man.

"No, I don't get it," I answer. "Can you help me understand?"

_____

I will pour out my thoughts to you; I will
make my words known to you.

Proverbs 1:23

| *Laundry Is Sexy—Part 1* |

The warmth of sheets and towels hot out of the dryer. The silky feel of dainties and intimate articles of apparel. The smell of bleach on newly laundered clothes....

Laundry is sexy.

Now if only I can convince you of this.

"The vines are in blossom; they give forth fragrance. Arise, my love, my fair one, and come away."

Song of Songs 2:13

Gratitude

I get home from an especially hard day at work. I'd love some sympathy, some comfort, some gratitude, but all I hear about are the kids, the kids, the kids.

"Look," I say. "I don't need to hear this. I've just spent ten hours working. You'd think I'd get a thank-you."

As soon as the words are out, I regret them.

The fool says, "I have no friends, and I get no thanks for my good deeds. Those who eat my bread are evil-tongued." How many will ridicule him, and how often!
Sirach 20:16-17

> Family System

Each of us is the product of a family system. We were affected by the family culture we grew up in. We bring all of these influences with us to our marriage, and many of our feelings and reactions may come from associations with the past and not from what we have together now.

When I find myself being depressed or harboring feelings of oppression, I need to look to the sum total of our life together for the good things we are to each other, not to the old patterns that I inherited.

"Your father made our yoke heavy. Now therefore lighten the hard service of your father and his heavy yoke that he placed on us."

1 Kings 12:4

| I Hate You |

I hate you because you hurt me.

I hate you because I am hurt.

I hate you because I love you.

I hate you because you have the power to touch me in ways no one else can.

I hate you because I give you this power.

I give you this power because I love you.

Power belongs to God, and steadfast love belongs to you, O Lord.
Psalm 62:11-12

Beneath the Surface

Outside the world is frozen, covered with white blowing snow. Mother Nature's cold blasts have cancelled work, meetings, errands and trips. Life has slowed to a standstill.

But sometimes what appears on the surface as frozen inactivity masks burgeoning life and new growth underneath.

I pull out the Scrabble game that we used to play all the time when we were first married, and we rekindle a pleasure we have not enjoyed in months—or is it years?

While nature plays outside, you and I play inside.

Do two walk together unless they have made an appointment?

Amos 3:3

> *Wonderful Invention*

There is a part of me that cowers in the fear that you will reject me, even after all these years. I rush to explain; I get louder and louder; you back away.

Only later do I remember that you love me even when I'm a jerk.

Marriage is such a wonderful invention!

But I, through the abundance of your steadfast love, will enter your house.

Psalm 5:7

Reminders

"It's okay to indulge once in a while. Go ahead, buy yourself a little cologne. So what if it's not on sale?"

"But we don't have the money."

"I know, but you are worth it. I just wanted to remind you of that."

"You remind me of that every day."

"When the bow is in the clouds, I will see it and remember the everlasting covenant between God and every living creature of all flesh that is on the earth."

Genesis 9:16

Second Fiddle

I'm jealous of all those people who call on the phone and interrupt our dinners and conversations. I'm jealous because you drop everything to come to the aid of your family and friends and coworkers. I'm jealous because it seems they are more important to you than I am.

Just because I'm always here, doesn't mean I'll always be here. Just because I'm not in a crisis, doesn't mean I don't need you just as much as they do.

I didn't marry you to play second fiddle to anyone.

So be careful not to forget the covenant that the LORD your God made with you, and not to make for yourselves an idol in the form of anything that the LORD your God has forbidden you. For the LORD your God is a devouring fire, a jealous God.
Genesis 4:23-24

A Few Beers

A few beers never hurt anybody. I bring home a paycheck every week. I haven't missed a day's work in years. How can she complain about a few beers?

He goes for those beers before he goes for me. Hardly a "hello, how was your day?" before heading for the refrigerator. He plops himself in front of the TV. He doesn't spend any time with the kids.

What's a few beers? After all, my dad always had a few beers each night. What's the big deal?

Sometimes I think he loves beer more than me and the kids.

"You are to distinguish between the holy and the common, and between the unclean and the clean."

                                        Leviticus 10:10

What the Experts Say

The experts say, "Always make your marriage your first priority."

The experts say, "Schedule time together, fix romantic meals, write poems to each other."

The experts say, "Meet your spouse at the door, the kids in bed or safely spirited away at Grandma's, the house spotless, a rump roast in the oven, wearing nothing but a martini."

These "experts" never had our jobs or our kids.

And the angel said to me, "Write this: Blessed are those who are invited to the marriage supper of the Lamb." And he said to me, "These are true words of God."
                                        Revelation 19:9

Listen to What I Mean

Listen to what I mean,

    not what I say.

Sometimes I say the wrong thing

    or use the wrong words.

Sometimes you hear someone else talking,

    not me.

I don't mean to hurt you or offend you

    or sound just like your mother.

Please listen to what I mean,

    not what I say.

"Listen carefully to my words, and let my declaration be in your ears."

                    Job 13:17

On the Shelf

I'm putting my marriage on the shelf.

It's become another chore to me.

Do this. Don't do that.

Feel this. Don't feel that.

Feel that, but don't do it.

I'm tired of shoulds and oughts and expectations.

Why can't we just be friends and play in the
leaves together like kids?

Goodbye marriage.

Hello friend.

---

*This is my beloved and this is my friend, O
daughters of Jerusalem.*

Song of Songs 5:16

A Little Help

The words come out of our son's mouth quickly.

"Shut up, Dad."

"I love you, too," I tell him softly.

He turns to his mother. "That's not what I mean. Doesn't he know what I mean?" he says.

I look at his mother, my friend. Help me out here, my eyes ask.

You're doing just fine, hers respond.

---

*Then the L*ORD *God said, "It is not good that the man should be alone; I will make him a helper as his partner."*

Genesis 2:18

"Paying Bills"

It's Saturday morning. The kids are watching cartoons. We feed them their cereal and hurry back to bed to be alone together.

Coffee gets cold on the table as we embrace. It can be reheated later, after we cool off.

We hear a knock on the door and young hands, struggling to turn the locked doorknob.

"Go away," we say. "We're paying bills."

Saturday morning, paying bills.

———————————————

Make haste, my beloved, and be like a gazelle or a young stag upon the mountains of spices!

　　　　　　　　　　　　Song of Songs 8:14

Compromise—Part 1

He really would rather stay home. But in the end, after some badgering, he decided to go to the party with people from my workplace.

I appreciate that.

As it turns out, things were not as boring as he feared. He had fun, got a chance to be witty and all that. We both mingled, and soon it was time to leave.

Not so bad, he confessed on the way home.

I'm glad you could be there, I told him. And I am, even though we didn't get to spend much time with each other. Because I appreciate his willingness to compromise and do something for me.

Just as I hope I'd do the same for him.

"Do to others as you would have them do to you."

Luke 6:31

Prayer for Married Couples

Oh God of life, creator of us all,
> male and female,
>> guide and nurture all married couples.

Care for us with a tenderness beyond
> comprehension.

Provide us rest when we seek it,
> a push when we need it.

Give us strength to be faithful to
> you and to each other.

Plant the seed of your creativity
> within us.

---

*Have you not known? Have you not
heard? The LORD is the everlasting God,
the Creator of the ends of the earth. He
does not faint or grow weary; his understanding is unsearchable. He gives power
to the faint, and strengthens the powerless.*
> *Isaiah 40:28-29*

If God Does Not Bind

If God does not pervade a marriage, then the couple labors in vain. No amount of nights out or romantic trips or wishing it were so can keep together a relationship not held together by God.

If God does not bind, the relationship will not endure.

"What God has joined together...."

Unless the LORD builds the house, those who build it labor in vain. Unless the LORD guards the city, the guard keeps watch in vain. It is in vain that you rise up early and go late to rest, eating the bread of anxious toil.

Psalm 127:1-2

Running

She stopped drinking but she didn't stop running away from the pain that led her to drink in the first place.

He traded one addiction for another. From reading to religion to relationships, searching after the high that would "cure all" his unhappiness.

Those who wait for the Lord shall renew their strength, they shall mount up with wings like eagles, they shall run and not be weary, they shall walk and not faint.
Isaiah 40:31

It is her mouth that infuriates me. It used to be called "lip," this irreverence of hers.

"Don't give me any lip," I tell her.

So why is it, when I need consolation, that I seek solace from the kiss of her lips?

Your lips distill nectar, my bride; honey and milk are under your tongue.
                                                      Song of Songs 4:11

No Longer Alone

We sit together, my wife and I, and feast on roast turkey. She is unable to fit much into her stomach, compressed by the weight of the soon-to-be-born baby. She shares but a sip of wine with me. Already this little stranger has changed our lives. Already our baby's presence is felt among us.

I gaze at my spouse, awkwardly pushing back from the table, patting her large belly, and suddenly realize...

We are no longer alone.

"Whoever welcomes one such child in my name welcomes me."

Matthew 18:5

Supposed to Be

We both collapse in bed.

Our answering machines talk more than we do.
We leave notes to each other on the refrigerator as we
pass in the night from one responsibility to another.
More communication happens on our refrigerator door
than under our sheets.

And even when we manage a night out, we barely
find the energy to cut our meat before going home and
collapsing again.

This can't be the way marriage is supposed to be.

---

*Sow for yourself righteousness; reap
steadfast love; break up your fallow
ground; for it is time to seek the LORD, that
he may come and rain righteousness upon
you.*

Hosea 10:12

Laundry Is Sexy—Part 2

Time for lights out and the laundry is lumped on the blankets of our bed again.

"Help me fold," he says.

"Sure," I say.

The things are still warm. He turns them in his hands, smells them. Beautiful. He is beautiful. I would almost say laundry is sexy, but he would laugh at me.

"We can sneak their things into the kids' rooms," he says. "You know, while they're sleeping."

"No," I say, "leave them in the basket. Just this once. Okay?"

My beloved has gone down to his garden, to the beds of spices, to pasture his flock in the gardens, and to gather lilies. I am my beloved's and my beloved is mine; he pastures his flock among the lilies.
Song of Songs 6:2-3

There Is God

You are you, I am I.

We are separate, two distinct individuals.

We have a beginning and an end, limits, boundaries that define us and who we are.

You are you, I am I.

God is without limits, without end.

God transcends all human boundaries.

You are you, I am I.

Where we meet,

there is God.

So God created humankind in his image, in the image of God he created them; male and female he created them.

Genesis 1:27

Power Struggle

Oh, the subtle and not-so-subtle ways in which we try to manipulate each other to get our ways. Kill him with kindness, blow her away with flowers; give her the silent treatment, get the kids on his side—all to have our own ways, to make our spouses into the people we want them to be.

And if they still don't get the hint, we hide behind a wall of resentment and anger.

I don't want to play this game anymore.

---

*"But to what will I compare this genera-
tion? It is like children sitting in the
marketplaces and calling to one another,
'We played the flute for you, and you did
not dance; we wailed, and you did not
mourn.'"*

Matthew 11:16-17

Either / Or

Sometimes marriage is just a matter of survival. Putting up with each other's idiosyncracies and tantrums. Making it through the bad days and the bad times. Trusting that it will get better if we can just make it through this latest crisis.

Other times, marriage soars with the eagles. Discovering the other person's passions and genius. Living each day with the cup filled to overflowing. Waking up every morning looking forward to whatever adventure awaits.

Love is patient; love is kind; love is not envious or boastful or arrogant or rude. It does not insist on its own way; it is not irritable or resentful; it does not rejoice in wrongdoing, but rejoices in the truth. It bears all things, hopes all things, endures all things.

1 Corinthians 13:4-7

> ### Doesn't Come Cheap

Two may be able to live as cheaply as one, but you still pay a price. Marriage costs in terms of having to be accountable to another for how you spend your time and energy, in having to constantly risk being vulnerable with someone who knows you far too well.

Marriage doesn't come cheap. Its price is high. But then, there are no free lunches and you do get what you pay for.

"The kingdom of heaven is like a merchant in search of fine pearls; on finding one pearl of great value, he went and sold all that he had and bought it."

Matthew 13:45

I'm sorry for the times I grunted at you or ignored you when you walked in the door.

I'm sorry for the times I put the kids or my friends or my latest hobby first.

I'm sorry for the times I treated you like a big kid or just another responsibility.

I'm sorry if I clung too tightly.

I'm sorry for not always letting you know how important you are to me.

———————————————

Each of you, however, should love his wife as himself, and a wife should respect her husband.

Ephesians 5:33

Once Is Enough

She would hate to hear him think this out loud. But when it comes to housework, his thought always begins with, "My mother never used to do it this way."

He tried to say something once, and that was enough. So he keeps his thought to himself and tries to work around it.

Even fools who keep silent are considered wise; when they close their lips, they are deemed intelligent.

Proverbs 17:28

Threatened

I feel threatened when you notice the appearance of younger women. You see them at their best, dressed for the day, fresh and full of energy. You see me at my worst, tired from a long day, out of sorts with smeared makeup and barely enough energy to put the kids to bed.

I feel threatened because I'm getting older and I'm afraid I'll lose you to a younger, more exciting woman. I feel threatened because it has happened to so many other women I know. It could happen to me.

Are you kidding? I may be insensitive, but I'm not dumb. You are the best thing that ever happened to me, and I'm not about to blow it for some pop tart! You still ring my chimes and light my fire and every other cliché I can think of. I love you precisely because you are who you are...and I always will.

Now, about those rock stars you're always ogling....

> *Rejoice in the wife of your youth, a lovely deer, a graceful doe. May her breasts satisfy you at all times; may you be intoxicated always by her love.*
> *Proverbs 5:18-19*

$$\boxed{\textit{Good Idea}}$$

It's late. The children are asleep. You are asleep too, sitting in your chair. You snore and wake yourself with a start.

I look at you and laugh.

"Why don't you get up and go to bed?" I ask.

You look at me and smile. For a moment we are transported to another day, another time, when our love was yet new.

"Good idea," you say and reach for my hand.

Together we go upstairs.

I slept, but my heart was awake. Listen! my
beloved is knocking. "Open to me, my
sister, my love, my dove, my perfect one."
                                    Song of Songs 5:2

The Mysterious World of Women

"I want Mommy," she said.

"Well, Daddy's right here," I tell her.

She repeats the words, "I want Mommy."

"What does Mommy have that I don't?" I ask myself.

"Only Mommy can understand, because she's a girl," my daughter explains.

I don't get this mysterious world of women.

I call my wife at work.

"Help me understand," I ask her.

---

*Her children rise up and call her happy;
her husband too, and he praises her:
"Many women have done excellently, but
you surpass them all."*

Proverbs 31:28-29

What to Do?

I can tell the minute he walks in the door.

"Bad day, huh?" I ask.

"Gmmmm," he mumbles.

The ball's in my court now.

Do I baby him? Give him a cup of coffee and the paper and tell him to relax?

Do I sit and listen to his tales of trial like a good counselor?

Do I hit him with all my problems? "You think you've got it bad...?"

Do I give him the silent treatment, brush him off because I can't deal with him right now?

God, give me the wisdom to know what to do and the strength to do it.

"I give you a wise and discerning mind; no one like you has been before you and no one like you shall arise after you."
                                        1 Kings 3:12

Forged in Gold

I'm lying in bed awake. I remember so many other nights lying in bed, making love with you. We couldn't keep our hands off of each other. We couldn't bear to be separated for even a day.

I remember so many other nights lying in bed, making love with you. We couldn't keep our hands off of each other. We couldn't bear to be separated for even a day.

Our relationship is so much stronger now. It has withstood the strain of absence, the uncertainties of youth, even the fatigue of the ordinary.

Our marriage is solid, forged in gold.

In this you rejoice, even if now for a little while you have had to suffer various trials, so that the genuineness of your faith—being more precious than gold that, though perishable, is tested by fire—may be found to result in praise and glory and honor when Jesus Christ is revealed.

1 Peter 1:6-7

Making It Work

It's far easier to blame others for our marital problems: our kids, our friends, our in-laws, someone else...anyone else.

Maybe others do have their parts to play, but if we are honest we realize that we are the only two responsible for our relationship, and it is up to us to make it work.

The LORD God called to the man, and said to him, "Where are you?" He said, "I heard the sound of you in the garden, and I was afraid, because I was naked; and I hid myself." He said, "Who told you that you were naked? Have you eaten from the tree of which I commanded you not to eat?" The man said, "The woman whom you gave to be with me, she gave me fruit from the tree, and I ate." Then the LORD God said to the woman, "What is this that you have done?" The woman said, "The serpent tricked me, and I ate."

Genesis 3:9-13

God Is Love

I do not know God. The whole idea of a divine, transcendent being is just too grand for my little brain to comprehend.

But I do know you. And because of you I have experienced the power of love, a power greater than I ever imagined.

Thank you for giving me a glimpse of what God must be like.

No one has ever seen God; if we love one another, God lives in us, and his love is perfected in us.

1 John 4:12

Unemployed Husband

It's tough for a man being unemployed and trying to keep things together at home. She's off making a life for herself at work, and I'm home with the kids, preparing goody bags for our daughter's birthday party.

What's going on? I've got plans. I need to make connection with employers. There's this little project I've committed to. When am I going to have time to get my work done?

Sometimes I simply have to step back and tell myself, "Just listen to what you are saying." The whole time I was working, she was trucking kids around, cleaning, stuffing goody bags, dragging the kids with their earaches and runny noses to the doctors, and taking on little projects.

But what about making a living? I'm the one who is supposed to do that, aren't I?

"What sign are you going to give us then, so that we may see it and believe you? What work will you be performing?"

John 6:30

Most Certainly

I love you, but I'm scared. I can see the road behind but not the road ahead, and it scares me.

Will there be more pain, more loss? Most certainly.

Will there be hard times, misunderstandings, quarrels? Most certainly.

But will there be joy? Most certainly.

Will there be love? Most certainly.

Will it be worth it? Most certainly.

Do not fear, or be afraid; have I not told you from of old and declared it? You are my witnesses! Is there any god besides me? There is no other rock; I know not one.
Isaiah 44:8

$$\boxed{\textit{Bad Spells}}$$

We each have bad spells—bad days, bad weeks, bad months, even bad years when everything seems to go wrong, nothing works out the way we want it. The fact of our being married doesn't mean these bad periods always coincide.

One spouse's good days can help alleviate, or at least put into perspective, the other's bad days.

But when we both hit a bad spell together or when one partner's bad spell lasts too long, sometimes it helps to be together....

And sometimes it doesn't.

May the God of steadfastness and encour-
agement grant you to live in harmony with
one another, in accordance with Christ
Jesus, so that together you may with one
voice glorify the God and Father of our
Lord Jesus Christ.

Romans 15:5-6

Lingerie—why is he giving me lingerie? Is this a hint that our sex life isn't good?

"Oh, thank you. It's wonderful. You shouldn't have."

"But you're worth it, honey. Happy Valentine's Day."

She's lying. She doesn't really like it. Does she think I'm unhappy with our sex life? How could I be so dumb?

They go out to dinner. They talk. They dance. Later that night, she goes into the bathroom and puts on the gift and....

Every generous act of giving, with every perfect gift, is from above, coming down from the Father of lights, with whom there is no variation or shadow due to change.
James 1:17

> ## Love Story—Part 1

The elderly man was rolled into the room in a wheelchair. He sat close, but not too close, to the bed where a woman lay dying of cancer.

"Three times," he said to no one in particular. "Three times we divorced and remarried. We'd quarrel and she'd leave. Then one of us would get in trouble and the other would help out. Then we'd get back together. If only she'd get well enough, I'd take care of her again."

"Three times," he said. "She left me. But she always came back. This time she won't."

O Ephraim, what have I to do with idols? It is I who answer and look after you. I am like an evergreen cypress; your faithfulness comes from me.

Hosea 14:8

My son and I are looking through a magazine. The models are there in full force.

"Is Mommy beautiful?" he asks.

"Yes, your mom is beautiful," I answer, but I want to tell him more.

I want to tell him that beauty is more than skin deep, although his mother has beautiful skin.

I want to tell him that beauty only completely unfolds over time and that his mother gets more beautiful every day.

I want to tell him that there is something about his mother's beauty that bursts through the dull and the routine at the most unexpected moments.

But, hey, the kid is only six.

———————————

Ah, you are beautiful, my love; ah, you are beautiful; your eyes are like doves. Ah, you are beautiful, my beloved, truly lovely.
Song of Songs 1:15-16

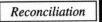

Reconciliation

Can we love again? I don't know. Do we dare try?

Have we worked out the problems from the past or will they reappear as soon as the glow is off the reconciliation? Are we doomed for failure, to consistently repeat our mistakes?

Will we fall back into old patterns as quickly as we fall back into bed? Have we truly changed and can we make it work?

Dare we try?

Be serious and discipline yourselves for the sake of your prayers. Above all, maintain constant love for one another, for love covers a multitude of sins.
1 Peter 4:7-8

What I Really Wish

When I think about our problems and look at some of the other couples around us, I get depressed. Everyone else's marriage looks so good.

What I wouldn't give to know that they have bad moments of their own. But then I have to stop myself. I would not want to wish our difficulties on anyone, and I would not want us to have to deal with theirs.

What I really wish is that you and I could always face our momentary crises with grace, goodwill and love.

———————

The fruit of the Spirit is love, joy, peace, patience, kindness, generosity, faithfulness, gentleness, and self-control.
                                        Galatians 5:22

Knowledge and Feeling

There is something to be said for knowing, for intellectual knowledge; and there is something equally important to be said for feeling, for emotional knowledge.

If I only knew then what I know now, I could have prepared myself for reality. It seems as if my dreams have fled and I am far away from where we were when we started.

If only I felt now what I felt then—that the world was ours and together we could make all our dreams come true. There was no end to my energy.

Help me to wed my present knowledge with my past feelings.

Dreams come with many cares.
Ecclesiastes 5:3

A Flower in Sunshine

Once in a while, it happens. I am transported to a place that is so right, so perfect, so wonderful. And you are there with me.

Our busy existence, the madness of its ever-quickening pace, is left far behind. All seems to slow down and to open up, like a flower in sunshine.

I reach out to hold your hand. There is nothing to say. You and I understand there would not be moments like this unless we were together.

Therefore a man leaves his father and mother and clings to his wife, and they become one flesh. And the man and his wife were both naked, and were not ashamed.
Genesis 2:24-25

Sexy—Part 1

You can have your pinups of men in leopard-skin racing trunks. Give me a man with spit-up on his collar. A man who's unkempt and unshaven, not from a night out with the boys but from a day at home with sick kids. A man who exhibits his virility through wrestling with six eight-year-olds at a birthday party or three kids and a grocery cart. A man whose idea of a night with the boys is playing cards with his sons.

That's my idea of sexy!

My soul is satisfied as with a rich feast, and my mouth praises you with joyful lips when I think of you on my bed, and meditate on you in the watcher of the night; for you have been my help, and in the shadow of your wings I sing for joy.

Psalm 63:5-7

Imperfection

There is no magical person who will fulfill all our needs and desires for relationship, a perfect match in all areas of our life. At most we are imperfect humans living imperfectly together, struggling through daily life toward a destiny we do not comprehend.

Beloved, we are God's children now; what we will be has not yet been revealed.

                                        1 John 3:2

Childhood Sweethearts

They met in grade school, exchanging insults on the playground. He pulled her hair. She stuck her gum on his seat in school, where it neatly lodged on his pants.

They were together in high school, sharing triumphs and disasters, hopes and dreams, romances and heartbreaks, always remaining "just friends."

They went away to different colleges and rarely communicated. They drifted apart to find new friends, new ideas, new challenges. Still, they called each other up whenever they were home for the holidays and found their friendship still alive.

Who knows when their friendship turned to love? Neither of them is sure. He now insists he loved her from the moment he first saw her; she's not so sure when it happened.

But one thing they are sure of now is that they will be together forever, for the rest of their lives—and beyond.

I loved her and sought her from my youth; I desired to take her for my bride.

Wisdom 8:2

Breakthrough

When you reach an impasse in a road, you have to go around it, go over it, go under it, or go a new way.

When you reach an impasse in your marriage, you have to do the same. Develop new friends, new interests, new ways of doing things.

And then will come the breakthrough.

"Thus says the LORD: This is how I will break the yoke of King Nebuchadnezzar of Babylon from the neck of all the nations within two years."

Jeremiah 28:11

| No Guarantees |

There are no guarantees in life. No guarantee that the child you raise won't become a drug addict. No guarantee that your job will still be there next year or that you'll have all the money you need throughout your retirement.

Children grow up and leave. Jobs come and go. Friends move away.

In a world full of uncertainties, he thought there was one thing he could count on. When he said "I do," he thought it meant she would always be with him.

Now he has learned a painful truth. It was only a lifetime guarantee.

For as all die in Adam, so all will be made alive in Christ.

                              1 Corinthians 15:22

In the Beginning

In the beginning God created male and female. Man plants the seed, but woman gives birth. There is no life without the seed, no life without a place to nurture the seed to maturity.

Which came first? Both came from the same life-source.

In the beginning there were two.

Two are better than one.

Ecclesiastes 4:9

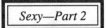

Sexy—Part 2

You can have your centerfolds—naked, airbrushed and polished for the page. Give me a woman in jeans and sweatshirt, with no time for makeup because she's up early after a night of studying and rushing to drive her sister-in-law to work.

A woman who exhibits her femininity through soothing the kids' ills and sharing her long day with me over a cup of tea—in the same jeans and sweatshirt because there is no time to change before she has to head out for class. Whose idea of a night with the girls is arranging a birthday party for our six-year-old and ten of her classmates.

A woman who rolls into bed and pulls me close so that, even though half asleep, I hear her say, "I love you."

———————————

Do not adorn yourselves outwardly by braiding your hair, and by wearing gold ornaments or fine clothing; rather, let your adornment be the inner self with the lasting beauty of a gentle and quiet spirit, which is very precious in God's sight.

1 Peter 3:3-4

Fault

It was his fault. He neglected her for his job. He couldn't communicate.

It was her fault. She put the kids first. She wasn't honest enough.

It was their fault. They didn't value their marriage enough. They didn't try hard enough to work things out.

It was society's fault. There's too much pressure on families. The male/female roles are too blurred. There's too much temptation, too much acceptance of divorce.

The one who admits...fault will be kept from failure.

Sirach 20:3

> ## Anybody Home?

Hello, are you there? Is anybody home?

Sometimes you seem so distant, so far away. I don't know who you are anymore. I think I've lost you.

And then I find you again.

You are changed, and yet you remain the same wonderful person I married.

Listen, I will tell you a mystery! We will not all die, but we will all be changed.
1 Corinthians 15:51

Too Hard

Was there a time when I pushed too hard, when I went too far?

I want to know, to set things straight.

If ever I asked you to do something you did not want to do, forgive me. I wouldn't like myself if I ever hurt you like that.

Have you sinned, my child? Do so no more but ask forgiveness for all your past sins.
Sirach 21:1

> ## What Is It?

Men fascinate me. What is it about them? They strut about like peacocks or roosters in a chicken coop, picking fights to see who will end up on top. They peck and fight and come out buddies.

I've yet to figure them out, but it's sure fun trying!

––––––––––––

As an apple tree among the trees of the wood, so is my beloved among young men. With great delight I sat in his shadow, and his fruit was sweet to my taste.
Song of Songs 2:3

Missing You

I know you need to be gone. I know this trip is important to you. But it doesn't change the fact that I miss you.

I miss your kiss, your tender caress. I miss your smile and the way you make me laugh.

Say it won't be too long.

"Tomorrow is the new moon; you will be missed, because your place will be empty."

1 Samuel 20:18

Abuse—Part 1

She knows the wrath of an abusive partner. The physical abuse is bad enough, but the psychological trauma drives her to the brink.

She calls us after it happens, and we hear the fear in her voice. "Are you okay?" we ask. "Do you want to come over?" "No, I'll be all right," she says, but we know she won't.

We hang up and cling tightly to each other.

If you do abuse them, when they cry out to me, I will surely heed their cry.

Exodus 22:23

Mentor

I nod. He is my friend, in many ways my mentor.

His marriage is a model for my spouse and me.

He shares his insights, and he listens to me.

But one thing I've learned is that there is no replicating anyone else's relationship. Success in a relationship comes from the uniqueness of what two people have to offer each other in their own circumstances. Success means coming back to us, to our situation, to see how wisdom flows in and out, over and under, in and through each of us.

---

*If there is any encouragement in Christ,
any consolation from love, any sharing of
the Spirit, any compassion and sympathy,
make my joy complete: be of the same
mind, having the same love, being in full
accord and of one mind.*

Philippians 2:1-2

The Catch

She wants more kids. They already have two, and two is enough for him. He doesn't feel that he gives the children enough time as it is—even though he considers himself a family man. Besides, his career is just taking off, and the house needs a lot of attention.

But there she is. He married her because he wanted to make her happy.

How will another child affect what they already have? How will not having another child affect them?

That's the catch.

I have been young, and now am old, yet I have not seen the righteous forsaken or their children begging bread. They are ever giving liberally and lending, and their children become a blessing.

Psalm 37:25-26

Better Than This

They watch the sun rise on their balcony each morning and go for long walks on the beach every evening. Sometimes they talk, most times they are silent.

After years of raising kids and working hard, after seeing their children married and raising children of their own, they've earned their trips to far-off places.

It doesn't get better than this.

Come, my beloved, let us go forth into the fields, and lodge in the villages; let us go out early to the vineyards, and see whether the vines have budded, whether the grape blossoms have opened, and the pomegranates are in bloom. There I will give you my love.

Song of Songs 7:11-12

To Each His / Her Own

A night out with the boys. A night of watching sports, cussing, drinking beer, smoking cigars, and telling war stories or tall tales about the one that got away.

I don't see what he sees in it.

A hen party. A night of gossiping, exchanging recipes, sipping wine, sampling desserts, and bragging about their kids.

I don't see what she sees in it.

"Good night, dear, have a good time."

"You, too, honey."

For everything created by God is good,
and nothing is to be rejected, provided it is
received with thanksgiving; for it is
sanctified by God's word and by prayer.
1 Timothy 4:4-5

> *Marriage Is Difficult*

Parenting is an everchanging job. As soon as you think you've got one stage conquered, along comes another challenging you to adjust and fine-tune your parenting skills.

Marriage is also ever changing. While the changes may not be as apparent as the obvious growth from infant to childhood to teen to young adult, they are there nonetheless, requiring constant attention.

What makes marriage more difficult than child rearing is that both parties are changing at different times and different rates, with neither having the age or experience to provide any perspective, and neither having the authority to make decisions or the wisdom to offer compromise.

Neither seek what is too difficult for you,
nor investigate what is beyond your power.
Reflect upon what you have been com-
manded, for what is hidden is not your
concern.

Sirach 3:21-22

> Shared Prayer

I share with you my life, my love, my body, my feelings. Dare I share my prayers?

I'm not talking about formal prayers at meal time or church. I mean how I talk with God when no one else is watching...or listening.

Dare I share that level of intimacy with you?

———————————————

The Spirit helps us in our weakness; for we do not know how to pray as we ought, but that very Spirit intercedes with sighs too deep for words.

Romans 8:26

> ### When She's Away

Our little boy can't calm down, so we call his mom on the phone at work. Somehow she makes him feel relaxed, confident, content.

I'm both happy and sad—happy that she is able to solve the immediate crises, sad that I don't seem to be able to help him when she's away.

Do not be far from me, for trouble is near and there is no one to help.

Psalm 22:11

Confession

The ninth step of the twelve steps of AA says that we make direct amends to people wherever possible, except when to do so would injure them or others.

We all need to confess our failings to another at times. Sometimes in our need to get something "off our chest," however, we may harm someone else needlessly.

I may be your friend and lover, but I'm not your confessor. Some secrets are too hard for me to bear. They hold too much hurt. They require forgiveness I may not be ready or able to give.

If you need confession—see a priest.

_____

When deeds of iniquity overwhelm us, you forgive our transgressions.

Psalm 65:3

Finding What Was Lost

What happened to the woman he married? That woman had been strong and independent. This woman was dependant and afraid. She hid behind the children until it seemed she no longer knew how to function in the adult world. Her life was the kids and there was no room for him.

Where was the girl he had married? How had he lost her? Was she still there, somewhere? And could he find her again?

---

*We are not among those who shrink back
and so are lost, but among those who have
faith and so are saved.*

Hebrews 10:39

> ### No-Win Situation

If I'm strong and independent, then you don't feel needed. If I'm weak and dependent, then I'm clinging, smothering. If I try to help you, I'm mothering you. If I don't help you, then I'm uncaring.

No matter what I do, I lose.

Since it is by God's mercy that we are engaged in this ministry, we do not lose heart.

2 Corinthians 4:1

The Decision

They had made all of the important decisions together. When they had decided to marry, it was a mutual decision. She didn't decide on her own to go out and get pregnant. They chose that together. They chose together where they would live, what cars to buy, where to send the kids to school.

But this decision—his decision to leave—would be made alone. And she would have no choice but to accept with as much grace and dignity as she could muster.

He stands alone and who can dissuade him? What he desires, that he does.

Job 23:13

Stress

He can tell when she is feeling stress. She starts to yell at the kids. She can't seem to get anything done, and there's always more to do. Even if she does get something done, there's always more to do. Even if she does get something done, it's not enough. He wants to tell her to relax, take it slow, take it one job at a time.

But who is he to tell her how to behave? So he tries to help out a little more, maybe take the kids outside while she collects herself, do a few of the tasks she has laid out for herself.

But there are things he wants to do too. So he catches himself raising his voice to the children, trying to do too much himself, and feeling as if he is being used.

She can tell that he is feeling stress, so she tries to help out a little more....

For the sake of my relatives and friends I will say, "Peace be within you." For the sake of the house of the LORD our God, I will seek your good.

Psalm 122:8-9

Other Couples

Oh, how I love to watch other couples together. Young lovers, holding hands or even quarrelling. Old lovers, sitting in comfortable silence forged through years of relationships or even picking at each other in ways that work only for them.

I wonder what people see when they observe you and me together.

I saw the holy city, the new Jerusalem,
coming down from heaven from God,
prepared as a bride adorned for her
husband.

                                        Revelation 21:2

Passion—Part 1

What is the true passion of marriage? Is it heated arguments followed by torrid lovemaking? Is it constant uncertainty, wondering if the one you love feels the same way? Is it jealousy or wanting to be with your beloved every moment of every day? Is it the inability to keep your hands off of each other?

Or is it the passion of childbirth, bearing down together to produce new life? Is it encouraging each other to hang in there during the down times in life? Is it a passion that waits, that isn't afraid that time or distance will kill it? Is it a passion born out of friendship?

Set me as a seal upon your heart, as a seal upon your arm; for love is as strong as death, passion fierce as the grave. Its flashes are flashes of fire, a raging flame.
Song of Songs 8:6

Stability

Marriages need stability. There is something safe and secure in knowing you will always be there for me and I will always be there for you. But marriages also thrive on a little excitement, a little adventure, a little mystery.

Stability is just the grounding from which our relationship takes wing!

"You have seen what I did to the Egyptians, and how I bore you on eagles' wings and brought you to myself. Now therefore, if you obey my voice and keep my covenant, you shall be my treasured possession out of all the peoples."

Exodus 19:4-5

| Loneliness |

There is no worse loneliness than that of two married people living together as strangers. The loneliness is greater precisely because of the promise of togetherness and love with which they started.

———————————————

Where then is my hope? Who will see my hope? Will it go down to the bars of Sheol? Shall we descend together into the dust?
Job 17:15-16

Something's Wrong

They say that men form relationships in order to have sex and women have sex in order to form relationships. Both tolerate the other in order to have what they want.

Something's wrong here.

"I give you a new commandment, that you love one another. Just as I have loved you, you also should love one another."
                                                    John 13:34

Tapestry

In Homer's *The Odyssey*, Penelope worked at her loom while awaiting Ulysses' return. By day she worked, by night she took apart what she had done in the day so that she would not finish until he came home.

Marriage can be like a tapestry woven by two people. If there is a flaw in the early weavings, you sometimes have to take everything apart in order to correct it and begin again. Some weaves don't work, others do. What works for some couples doesn't work for others. But always there must be two weavers.

How goes the work of art we are creating?

A new creation is everything!

Galatians 6:15

Happy Again

The car bottoms out on the speed bump in the church parking lot. We turn to see them, an older couple, married now—one after a divorce and the other after her first husband died.

They wave happily, happy to be together, happy to be seen together. Their old boat of a car lists, straightens itself, and cruises by us out onto the main drag and away.

"You have made known to me the ways of life; you will make me full of gladness with your presence."

Acts 2:28

| *Light My Fire* |

Is the spark gone? Has it been buried under laundry, dirty dishes and fussy kids? Was it quenched by years of job changes, financial crises, health crises and family crises?

It's hard to feel a flame when we are awash with worry and stress.

Come on, baby, light my fire.

He brought me to the banqueting house,
and his intention toward me was love.
Sustain me with raisins, refresh me with
apples; for I am faint with love.
                    Song of Songs 2:4-5

First Class

She likes secondhand clothes, furniture from garage and estate sales, mildly or slightly used appliances. She's never paid full price for brand new anything, even when we had the money. Too extravagant, she says. She takes second best and makes them look first rate.

She even takes him when he's feeling down and makes him feel first class.

You shall be happy, and it shall go well with you. Your wife will be like a fruitful vine within your house.

Psalm 128:2-3

| The Phoenix |

Society is changing. The institution of marriage is changing. Out of the rubble will come the phoenix, but first we must have the rubble.

———————————

"See, I am making all things new."
                    Revelation 21:5

Room to Grow

Traditionally men have sought to control through the use of force and domination and women through wiles, guilt and manipulation, although there are plenty of manipulative men and dominating women. Both strategies are ways of trying to exert one's will over one's spouse.

But relationships don't flourish when one partner or the other is in control. Relationships flourish when both husband and wife have freedom and room to grow.

Suddenly there was an earthquake, so violent that the foundations of the prison were shaken; and immediately all the doors were opened and everyone's chains were unfastened.

Acts 16:26

Kiss-and-Tell

Anybody who's anybody, and even somebodies who are relative nobodies, are writing their kiss-and-tell autobiographies. We know in lurid detail every tiny aspect of their real and imagined romances. We learn more than we really want to know about these people.

I like the fact that nobody but you and I know about our love life.

"Let the one who boasts, boast in the Lord."

1 Corinthians 1:31

Meteorologist of Marriage

Around here, March comes in like a lion and goes out like a lamb. I wish the same could be said about our disagreements, so that the duration and outcome could be anticipated with the same certainty as the weather!

I suppose if I were to be a meteorologist of marriage I would consult indicators, patterns, the history of our storms.

But who has the time? We are busy living. Come live with me and be my love, through disagreements and reconciliation alike.

Let the lion lie down with the lamb in each of us, so we may lie down with each other.

Then they cried to the LORD in their trouble, and he brought them out from their distress; he made the storm be still, and the waves of the sea were hushed.
              Psalm 107:28-29

> *Resurrection*

Easter celebrates Jesus' victory over despair and failure. He experienced the worst that human existence has to offer—betrayal, injustice, pain, degradation and death—yet God raised him above it to eternal life. Love conquered all.

Married couples can experience the worst of human existence as well. We too can know betrayal, injustice, pain, degradation and death, and we too can overcome these with the help of God. Love can conquer all.

In the midst of our worst despair and failure, let us believe in and anticipate our resurrection.

"I am the resurrection and the life. Those who believe in me, even though they die, will live, and everyone who lives and believes in me will never die."
                                    John 11:25-26

> *Tender Mercies*

How does God bind a man and a woman together for life? It isn't just by physical passion, although that's one of the most pleasant ways. It's also through a word here, a kindness there; one person going out of the way for the other even when he or she really doesn't want to. It is in both partners wishing for and wanting the other's happiness first.

God doesn't bind a man and woman only with passion. It takes a lifetime of tender mercies.

For their sake he remembered his covenant,
and showed compassion according to the
abundance of his steadfast love.
                                    Psalm 106:45

> ### The Wind

The wind blows where it will. It comes when least expected and goes without notice. Sometimes it's a gentle breeze, sometimes a shaking storm.

I try to lasso the wind but it slips away from me.

It's hard loving the wind.

"The wind blows where it chooses, and you hear the sound of it, but you do not know where it comes from or where it goes. So it is with everyone who is born of the Spirit."
John 3:8

Illusions

Illusions of control:

1. that I can control you—what you think,
   how you feel;

2. that you can control me—how I feel,
   what I think;

3. that we can control our lives—
   what happens to us,
   the consequences of our decisions.

The only one in control is the One who gives us
the freedom and power we exercise and enjoy.

---

*I know, O Lord, that the way of human
beings is not in their control, that mortals
as they walk cannot direct their ways.*
                              Jeremiah 10:23

The Unthinkable—Part 1

They are only a few years older than we.

Their kids go to school with ours.

They just found out he has terminal cancer.

We should be praying for them.

Offering to do whatever we can to help.

Instead, we're thinking about ourselves.

———————————————

*"Keep awake therefore, for you know
neither the day nor the hour."*

Matthew 25:13

Secrets were meant to be shared with the one you trust the most.

What are your secrets, those deep, dark, hidden episodes you've never shared?

I'll trust you with mine, if you trust me with yours.

_____

Whatever you have said in the dark will be heard in the light, and what you have whispered behind closed doors will be proclaimed from the housetops.

Luke 12:3

I don't love you because I need you.

I need you because I love you.

---

*Now that you have purified your souls by
your obedience to the truth so that you
have genuine mutual love, love one another
deeply from the heart.*

                                        1 Peter 1:22

Pride

There are times I sit back, knowing she's got to handle things herself.

There is yelling, and I can't believe the kids are better for it. I grew up in a house of yellers. I can be a yeller too. So I suffer knowing she suffers because it's frustrating being a parent.

But then there are the times I overhear a conversation she is having with one of the kids, and it is filled with wisdom, and my heart leaps. Here is the woman I married—I am so proud of her.

As a mother comforts her child, so I will comfort you.

Isaiah 66:13

| Un-Adult-Erated Fun |

I wish we could enter so totally into play the way children do. Their worries are left behind. All they think of is the moment.

Sometimes I think we are too serious about life. Let's have some un-adult-erated fun.

The streets of the city shall be full of boys and girls playing in its streets.

Zechariah 8:5

Look at this world we live in. Some people say it's a mess and men made it that way. If women had been in charge it would have been different, they say.

"They" are right, you know. It would have been different...but not necessarily better. Women make as many mistakes as men, just different ones.

When will men and women learn to live with each other in equality and peace?

We need both sexes to compensate for each other's failings and weaknesses.

"This at last is bone of my bones and flesh of my flesh; this one shall be called Woman, for out of Man this one was taken."

Genesis 2:23

> ## Shooting Some Hoops

I've waited all day to grab a few minutes for myself. I used to think it was selfish to let things slide—things like the dishes or the laundry or making the bed. But I've learned that if I take a few minutes for myself—to center, to putter, to goof off—everything gets done eventually, and I'm a lot happier.

So when my spouse comes in the door, I am out into the bright sunlight to shoot basketballs, sweat, let my lungs work a little.

I feel renewed when I return home.

Restore in me the joy of your salvation,
and sustain in me a willing spirit.
Psalm 51:12

The Single Life

Sometimes I envy my single female friends. No one to answer to or pick up after. No stumbling over someone else's shoes, no never-ending battles over the toilet lid.

Sometimes I envy my single male friends. Nights out with the "boys," staying up as late as you want with nobody to answer to.

Marriage isn't all it's cracked up to be.

But, then again, we've played that tune before.

We've both tried the single life. Maybe it's more fun in our dreams than in reality.

The single life isn't all it's cracked up to be, either.

---

*The one who lives alone is self-indulgent,
showing contempt for all who have sound
judgment.*

                                        Proverbs 18:1

> ### More Energy

We are limited. God is unlimited. The energy we spend here means less energy for there. The energy we expend on the kids means less energy for work. The energy we put into our jobs means less energy for each other, and on and on.

But God is unlimited energy. If we can just tap into that...more energy for everything!

Great is our Lord, and abundant in power,
his understanding is beyond measure.
Psalm 147:5

Married, with Children

He doesn't like how she cooked the pot roast.

She doesn't like the way he does dishes.

He doesn't like her choice of TV programs.

She doesn't likes the way he "hogs" the paper.

Neither of them likes how the other one deals
with the kids.

They are "Married, with Children."

---

*"O how wretched am I and many times
unhappy!"*

4 Maccabees 16:6

Silent Bond

We reach across the table and silently hold hands.

If there is ever a time when we can't imagine *not* being married to each other, it's at times of sorrow like this.

When I thought, "My foot is slipping," your steadfast love, O LORD, held me up. When the cares of my heart are many, your consolations cheer my soul.

Psalm 94:18-19

Where Will We Be?

"Watch, she will keep talking and walk past the car," he says. He is in his eighties. They have been together fifty years. There is a twinkle in his eye as he cuts over and around to the driver's side of the car.

She continues her conversation with my wife and keeps going right down the row of cars. He pulls around and drives up in front of her.

She acts surprised. He laughs. They've probably played this game a million times.

I wonder what games we'll have perfected by the time we're their age?

Happy is the one who finds a friend.
Sirach 25:9

Passion—Part 2

What if Romeo and Juliet had escaped together? What would years of living have done to their love? Would their relationship have withstood the boredom of the ordinary? Would their marriage have lasted a lifetime? We'll never know.

Teenage love burns so hotly. "Foolish," "romantic," "unrealistic," the adult world says.

And yet there is something that draws us to that kind of passion.

Dare you and I explore it?

"Come, let us take our fill of love until morning; let us delight ourselves with love."

Proverbs 7:18

| Storms |

I love taking a walk during a storm. The raw energy unnerves me and invigorates me. The terrifying power of nature flails away, and I remember who I am—an insignificant human being in the midst of this terrible display of power. At one fell swoop I could be obliterated, blown away, destroyed. Yet I am not.

When we are in the midst of one of the storms in our life together, our words also have power. We have the power to obliterate each other. Remember, our real power is in healing. Our energy—electrical as it may be—is best exercised in forgiveness.

Now there was a great wind, so strong that it was splitting mountains and breaking rocks in pieces before the Lord, but the Lord was not in the wind; and after the wind was an earthquake, but the Lord was not in the earthquake; and after the earthquake a fire, but the Lord was not in the fire; and after the fire a sound of sheer silence.

1 Kings 19:11-12

> ## Intimate with Grief

She has buried two husbands. She knows full well the joys and sorrows of marital relationships. She has known the grief of losing a husband twice over, and yet she is willing to risk again. She has found love again in her "golden" years.

And she accepts that she may well know loss again.

Now I rejoice, not because you were grieved, but because your grief led to repentance; for you felt a godly grief, so that you were not harmed in any way.
2 Corinthians 7:9

A Moment—Part 1

It only took a moment—a glance, a look, the uncertainty of that first exchange. Dare he ask her for dinner? Should she take him to the movies?

Who made the very first move? They no longer remember.

He smiled. She laughed. Their fingers touched. They were somehow together, and they've been together ever since.

In a moment, in the twinkling of an eye.
1 Corinthians 15:52

Stages

Marriages go through stages of development.

There is the idealized, romantic love in the beginning.

Then comes the rough-edged love of getting beyond the ideal to the real, finding a way to live together that works for both of you, allowing each other the space to grow within the relationship and the freedom to come and go as you need.

And finally, there is the constant rapprochement when you come back together, changed and yet not changed, still in love and yet different from before.

From the wilderness of Sin the whole congregation of the Israelites journeyed by stages, as the LORD commanded.
Exodus 17:1

Judge and Jury

Who's to be the judge and jury over whether a marriage is "healthy" or not?

Well, how about God be the judge, and the couple be the jury?

He calls to the heavens above and to the earth, that he may judge his people: "Gather to me my faithful ones, who made a covenant with me by sacrifice!"
Psalm 50:4-5

| Water and Blood |

It gushes out, water and blood, a monthly reminder of my mortality—and of the potential for new life I constantly bear. Once a month, whether I like it or not, I'm confronted with this physical reality of womanhood.

A man has no counterpart to this, and therefore you can never completely understand how I feel about my body.

One of the soldiers pierced his side with a spear, and at once blood and water came out.

John 19:34

Love—Part 1

Love is blind.

Love too much.

In love.

Out of love.

Love too little.

Never-ending love.

Love at first sight.

Unrequited love.

Love of my life.

For everything there is a season, and a time for every matter under heaven...a time to love, and a time to hate.

Ecclesiastes 3:1, 8

Quarrels

"I don't love you and never have."

"You really aren't that important to me."

"I no longer care that much."

"Neither do I."

Who are we trying to kid? We love each other as much as ever.

And we're both always sorry after we fight.

Then why do we quarrel so?

Those conflicts and disputes among you,
where do they come from?

James 4:1

Companions

Marriage isn't a solution to the trials of life. You can't escape suffering, pain or aloneness through marriage. It isn't designed to give total meaning and purpose to the individuals involved. You must find that elsewhere.

But as we journey through this world, it's nice to have one special companion to share the road.

When I enter my house, I shall find rest
with her; for companionship with her has
no bitterness, and life with her has no pain,
but gladness and joy.

Wisdom 8:16

| Rough Edges |

Oh, how we bump and jostle each other. We come up against the rough edges in each of our lives— misunderstandings, miscommunications, unspoken expectations—and sometimes we get cut or rubbed raw.

Oh, how we jostle and bump each other until the edges are smoothed out.

Attack to the right! Attack to the left!
Wherever your edge is directed.
Ezekiel 21:16

The "Good-Enough" Spouse

What is a "good-enough" spouse? Is it someone who is just barely tolerable, someone who meets the bare minimum of acceptability?

Or is it a husband or wife who tries hard, who makes the best of his or her talents and opportunities, who is there for the other whenever it is truly necessary or important?

By that second definition, a "good-enough" spouse is good enough for me!

"Why do you call me good? No one is good but God alone."

Luke 18:19

> **Ball and Chain**

"The old ball and chain" is an obnoxious phrase. Men use it as a "humorous" excuse to keep them from doing something they don't really want to do anyway.

"The old ball and chain won't let me," they say.

Why isn't there an equivalently obnoxious phrase for women to use? How about "My husband, the electronic shackle operator, wants me at home"?

Whoever belittles another lacks sense, but an intelligent person remains silent.
Proverbs 11:12

After we married, I changed jobs several times and she supported me in my decisions, even though it meant material sacrifice. She has never wavered, although she has admitted things were tough.

I have been blessed by her understanding.

Have I told her that clearly enough?

You have turned my mourning into dancing; you have taken off my sackcloth and clothed me with joy, so that my soul may praise you and not be silent. O LORD my God, I will give thanks to you forever.
Psalm 30:11-12

Blooming

I have a flowering plant that hangs in a basket on our front porch. When I first got it, I left it outside one early spring night and almost lost it from the cold. Another day it was caught in a severe thunderstorm and violently tossed about. Once again I thought I had killed it, only to find that with a daily dose of water and sunshine it came back to life, producing an abundance of flowers.

Then it was left in my car during the heat of summer. This time I was sure it was gone, scorched by the sun's rays. But I carefully nursed it back to life and now it hangs on our front porch again, a little lopsided, a little worse for wear, but beautiful nonetheless.

Our marriage is like that plant. It can withstand the heat and cold and storms of life, but in order to blossom it needs water and sunshine—and love—on a daily basis.

Listen to me, my faithful children, and blossom like a rose growing by a stream of water.

Sirach 39:13

Mind Reading—Part 1

I'm not a mind reader, so don't expect me to know what you want. Don't expect me to jump at your least little grunt or look. Use the mouth God gave you to let me know what's going on inside.

I'm not a mind reader so don't expect me to be one. Don't pout when I don't fulfill your unspoken desires. If you expect me to do something, then tell me.

Discussion is the beginning of every work,
and counsel precedes every undertaking.
Sirach 37:16

What Goes Around

Staying home with kids wasn't your idea of a good time, but you did it.

When I needed to work overtime and weekends, you understood.

Now that you're working outside the home, it's my turn to take care of the children.

If you need extra time for work, you've got it.

How does that saying go? What goes around, comes around.

Indeed, you are faithful and true.
                                    3 Maccabees 2:11

Pushing You Away

I come home in a bad mood. I'm in a nowhere job, getting nowhere fast, and even this job may not last. Sometimes it feels as though the whole world is crumbling beneath my feet.

I come home and I snap at you over minor inconveniences. I see you turn away from me in fear and anger.

I snap at you when all I really want is to be held and comforted, reassured that your love will always be there.

When I need you the most, I push you away.

I do not understand my own actions. For I do not do what I want, but I do the very things I hate.

Romans 7:15

You have been working on some of your favorite projects, and I have been busy on some of my own.

The thought creeps in and sits on my shoulder like a bird. We are together after all these years, and I still love you.

Can I be this fortunate?

He who acquires a wife gets his best possession, a helper for him and a pillar of support.

Sirach 36:29

Fantasy and Reality

Fantasies are fun. They can make you do anything, be anybody, look any way you want. You can travel to exotic places, be wined and dined, make passionate love.

Fantasies are fun, but they're not real. They can't hold you close at night or help you with the housework by day.

I'm so glad we have both fantasy and reality.

———————————

Whom have I in heaven but you? And there is nothing on earth that I desire other than you.

Psalm 73:25

| Caught Up |

I get caught up in things. You know that. Don't trouble me with complexities, nuances, reasoned arguments; just get one task out of the way and let's move on to the next item.

I know that you get caught up in things. So I have to remind you to slow down, because you might be missing something.

Getting things done doesn't mean I'm insensitive or heartless. I just know there is plenty to do, and I don't want to get too far behind.

But you really don't want to ride roughshod over others. I can't let you ignore an important point, or hurt somebody's feelings.

There's so much to do.

And how you do it is important.

The Lord's servant must not be quarrel-some but kindly to everyone, an apt teacher, patient, correcting opponents with gentleness.
                                    2 Timothy 2:24-25

To Dream Again

I had so many dreams as a child, and even more as a teenager. You were to be the one who made my dreams come true, my prince charming, my knight in shining armor. I would be your lady fair, clothed in white, making everything right.

We met, we married, and those dreams were quickly put aside—crushed in the reality of day-to-day living.

Now it is time to dream again. New dreams. Better dreams. Dreams rooted in reality.

But this time we dream together, not alone.

"Listen to this dream that I dreamed."
Genesis 37:6

> ### Collision Course—Part 1

Thank God, I'm home. Can't wait to get out of this monkey suit and put my feet up. Just give me a few minutes to make the transition from work to home before being barraged by the kids and all that needs to be done.

Thank God, he's home. Our son has to be at basketball practice in ten minutes. What a day I've had. Just give me a short break from the kids, then I'll be ready to mother and wife again. The kids need to spend time with their dad, and they need to do it NOW!

Thank God, I'm home!

Thank God, he's home!

The people were filled with expectation, and all were questioning in their hearts.
Luke 3:15

Spring

Spring is in the air. Birds return, flowers bloom, and children are finally free from their prison of a house to play outside for hours. And we, their jailors, are free of a task we really don't want.

Spring is in the air. Come lie with me, my love. We'll lock the door and listen to the sounds of birds chirping and children playing in the distance.

Spring is in the air.

For you were called to freedom, brothers and sisters; only do not use your freedom as an opportunity for self-indulgence, but through love become slaves to one another.
Galatians 5:13

> *Appreciation—Part 1*

Discovering and rediscovering what it is I love and appreciate about you is not an exercise in imagination. It is merely a matter of careful listening and observation.

I will meditate on your precepts, and fix my eyes on your ways.

Psalm 119:15

| Green Grass |

The grass is always greener in the neighbor's yard...until you take a closer look. The women are always sexier, more exciting; the men more considerate and devoted husbands and fathers.

It can be tempting to go out and buy a whole new yard, replete with house and garage, rather than tend to and fertilize the one you already have.

The wicked covet the proceeds of wicked-ness, but the root of the righteous bears fruit.

Proverbs 12:12

Roller Blade

Come, roller blade with me, my love.

I know we're too old for such nonsense. I know we may fall. I know we will make fools of ourselves. I know what the neighbors will say.

Come skate with me, my love.

There are far too few days such as these left for us. Be foolish just this once. Be carefree again with me.

The nursing child shall play over the hole of the asp, and the weaned child shall put its hand on the adder's den.

Isaiah 11:8

Tolerance

In marriage we obviously have to practice tolerance. There are a multitude of minor irritations, annoying habits, mannerisms and idiosyncracies that must be overlooked by both partners if the marriage is to work.

Too much tolerance, however, can be a bad thing. Think about it: We "tolerate" those people whom we feel it is not worth our time and energy to confront.

We can't "tolerate" our spouses when they really need to look at what they are doing. If we—their husbands or wives—won't confront them, who will?

I will be silent no longer concerning their ungodly acts that they impiously commit, neither will I tolerate their wicked practices.

2 Esdras 15:8

Love—Part 2

We all want it. We search for it. But the most we can get is a glimmer of it, appearing unexpectedly, sometimes despite ourselves.

It is the love that gives endlessly without demands, that never tires, that's unfailing and unflinching.

But because we are human, we fail. Human love always places demands and receives demands in return. Even the love of a parent or grandparent places some demands on the children.

We can't give endlessly to another without any demand in return. To look for unconditional love in a relationship is to seek to return to the womb.

Human love is but a glimmer of divine love.

Let us consider how to provoke one another to love.

Hebrews 10:24

The better we define ourselves the more we help those around us define themselves. Being "different," then, is good.

So, please, give me permission to be myself. If anything, fight harder to be yourself. That way we will be helping each other be the persons we were meant to be.

You were taught...to be renewed in the spirit of your minds, and to clothe your-selves with the new self, created according to the likeness of God in true righteousness and holiness.

Ephesians 4:22-24

One Step at a Time

Step by step, without our even seeing it, we walk away from each other. Step by step, further afield we stray, until it seems we are observing each other from two different worlds.

How do we get back together? How do we learn to walk together once again?

That's easy: step by step, one step at a time.

You are no longer walking in love.
Romans 14:15

A Lifetime

Some say that marriage for a lifetime was a valid idea when the average life span was only forty years. But how can people stay together and stay in love through the uncharted waters of middle and old age? Aren't they sure to be bored out of their minds after twenty or thirty years of marriage?

We say no! There is more than enough mystery in exploring our relationship to last for two lifetimes, even if those lifetimes span a hundred years each.

"They are no longer two, but one flesh. Therefore what God has joined together, let no one separate."

Mark 10:8-9

> *Longing*

It's been too long, my friend. Too long since we've touched, too long between kisses. I long to hold you, long to feel you close to me, long for the time when we'll be one again.

For I am longing to see you so that I may share with you some spiritual gift to strengthen you—or rather so that we may be mutually encouraged by each other's faith, both yours and mine.

Romans 1:11

Seven-Layer Cake

Marriage can be like a seven-layer cake, each layer different from the first, each richer than the last.

When the layer of dew lifted, there on the surface of the wilderness was a fine flaky substance, as fine as frost on the ground. When the Israelites saw it, they said to one another, "What is it?" For they did not know what it was. Moses said to them, "It is the bread that the LORD has given you to eat."

Exodus: 16:14-15

Forgiveness

My forgiveness doesn't require anything of you. It doesn't require your apology or that you change. It does require something of me—that I change in some way. I must recognize my hurt and understand my own role in being hurt or my own helplessness in the situation.

This is a very active stance toward life, and an important strength in our relationship.

God doesn't ask us to be passive victims. God only asks us to forgive.

"Do not judge, and you will not be judged; do not condemn, and you will not be condemned. Forgive, and you will be forgiven."

Luke 6:37

Fickle Friend

Eros is a fickle friend. He lights where he will, disappears at a moment's notice. He appears when least expected, to our surprise and sometimes embarrassment.

Eros is a fickle friend, but our friend he is. He brings pleasure and excitement into our lives. He teaches us things about love we never knew.

Welcome, our fickle friend. Please stay a while.

Eat, friends, drink, and be drunk with love.
Song of Songs 5:1

Fifty-Fifty

Marriage isn't a fifty-fifty affair. Marriage requires one hundred percent—on both sides.

Steadfast love and faithfulness will meet; righteousness and peace will kiss each other.

Psalm 85:10

Emily Dickenson said she knew something was poetry when it took off the top of her head.

Sometimes, when the light catches your face in a certain way or when you laugh at something only you and I think is funny, you take off the top of my head.

Their eyes saw his glorious majesty, and
their ears heard the glory of his voice.
                              Sirach 17:13

> ### I Want More

I want more than a warm body to snuggle up to on cold winter nights.

I want more than someone to share chores and childrearing.

I want more than a good set of genes with which to procreate.

I want you...all of you.

I will most gladly spend and be spent for you. If I love you more, am I to be loved less?

                    2 Corinthians 12:15

Looking Back—Part 1

Do you ever look back and wonder what might have been?

What if we hadn't met? Had married other people? Had remained single all our lives?

Would we have been happier and more fulfilled? Is there something great we might have done or experienced? Somebody else we might have loved?

Personally, I don't care what we've missed. What we've got is good enough.

"No one who puts a hand to the plow and looks back is fit for the kingdom of God."
                                        Luke 9:62

| Modern Couple |

I'm a woman of today. I don't anticipate your every need. I don't thank you for help around the house or with the kids because, after all, it's your home and they're your kids too. Why should I be the one expected to do everything?

I'm a man of today. I share the housework and childrearing. Fifty-fifty, isn't that how it's supposed to be? We both bring home paychecks. We share the household tasks. Tit for tat, you wash my back and I'll wash yours.

Still, there's something missing in our relationship.

I wonder what it is?

---

*Love one another with mutual affection;
outdo one another in showing honor. Do
not lag in zeal, be ardent in spirit.*
                              Romans 12:10-11

Wanting Out

I want out. This marriage is no longer working. Certainly not for me. How could it be working for you?

I want out. I feel trapped, unappreciated, unloved. This isn't what I bargained for.

The bad times feel endless. I don't know how much more I can take.

Honey, I want out. Please listen to me.

Give me a reason to stay.

Please.

Wife, for all you know, you might save your husband. Husband, for all you know, you might save your wife.

1 Corinthians 7:16

> ### The Rest

I can't make up for all you didn't have in your childhood. I can't compensate for all you don't have at your job. I can't give you the sense of self-worth and self-esteem you never received as a child.

I can only love you as you are and hope that you can accept my love.

You and God will have to do the rest.

May he grant you your heart's desire, and fulfill all your plans. May we shout for joy over your victory, and in the name of our God set up our banners. May the Lord fulfill all your petitions.

Psalm 20:4-5

The Monthly Visitor

I've learned to pay attention when the "monthly visitor" comes along. It's important that I do, not because of the emotional swings she has, but because I like to be first in my wife's eyes. I want her attention and I want it now. So when her period arrives, I have to remember to put her first, to be aware of her needs, of her feelings, of her person.

Isn't it strange that I would need a monthly reminder to think about someone else, especially the person I love most?

I remember the devotion of your youth,
your love as a bride, how you followed me
in the wilderness, in a land not sown.
                    Jeremiah 2:2

Never ask a man to help you with a home-repair job. He will automatically do it himself rather than take the time to show you how.

Never ask a woman for advice on how to handle a screaming baby. She will automatically pick the child up herself and take over rather than watch you fumble.

It has something to do with male ego.

It has something to with female ego.

"For all who exalt themselves will be humbled, and those who humble themselves will be exalted."
                                    Luke 14:11

Generations

Since the first man and woman, children have been growing older, leaving home and marrying. Marriage is the basic engine of society.

How our ancestors throughout the centuries lived their marriage vows, for better or for worse, affect our marriages today. How we live out our marriage commitments today, whether renewed in love or simply tolerating each other's presence, will affect future generations.

We remember those who have gone before us in marriage for what they have taught us, and we commit ourselves to better our own relationships for what we will thereby teach future generations.

Your ancient ruins shall be rebuilt; you shall raise up the foundations of many generations; you shall be called the repairer of the breach, the restorer of streets to live on.

Isaiah 58:12

> *Words*

Yes.
  Yes.
    Yes.

Sometimes the words rise up
  and have to be spoken.

Thank you.
  Thank you.
    Thank you.

Sometimes the words rise up
  and have to be spoken.

I love you.
  I love you.
    I love you.

Sometimes the words rise up
  and have to be spoken.

---

*See, the former things have come to pass,
and new things I now declare; before they
spring forth, I tell you of them.*

Isaiah 42:9

These are the mornings I love.

The kids are sleeping in and we, busy couple that we are, have time together—to chat, to dream, to make love, to share our stories. And we do all of it.

I feel guilty.

Almost.

The mandrakes give forth fragrance, and over our doors are all choice fruits, new as well as old, which I have laid up for you, O my beloved.

Song of Songs 7:13

♦

Choices

They seemed to have everything: a house they built, two fancy foreign cars, no kids, unlimited income, exotic trips. But after five years of marriage they divorced.

We laughed because we didn't have anything—a rented apartment, one compact American car, three kids, vacations in the backyard—but we're still together and happy.

We're not better than the other couple. We just made better choices...at least for us.

Choose life so that you and your descendants may live, loving the LORD your God, obeying him, and holding fast to him; for that means life to you and length of days.
Deuteronomy 30:19-20

Talk, Talk, Talk

We talk about what happened during the day. We talk about the kids and what's going on in their lives. We talk about the neighbors, local gossip. We talk about world events.

But we never really talk about us.

We never talk about what's happening inside.

"Should a multitude of words go unanswered, and should one full of talk be vindicated? Should your babble put others to silence, and when you mock, shall no one shame you?"

Job 11:2-3

The Male Period

Why aren't men subjected to the "monthly visitor"? Then whenever they are in one of their "moods" they could blame their "periods." When they get cranky or bloated or have headaches, we'd know it was just "that time of the month" and pay no attention—just like they do to us.

Men can be every bit as moody and irrational as women. It's just not as regular and predictable!

Tell the older men to be temperate, serious, prudent and sound in faith, in love, and in endurance....Likewise, urge the younger men to be self-controlled.
Titus 2:2, 6

Desire

I look at you, my love,

and desire springs eternal.

I want the heat of you beside me,

the hunger of my longing satisfied.

I am my beloved's, and his desire is for me.
                    Song of Songs 7:10

Rut—Part 1

We're in a rut, we two.

Rut, what rut? There's something different on TV every night. We go out every Friday. Saturday is bowling night and Sunday is spent with family, yours or mine. Where's the rut?

Listen to yourself: the same place, the same people, the same routine.

What do you want? Shall we do something wild and crazy like skydiving or white water rafting?

Nothing as drastic as that. How about the next time we eat out, we forego dinner and go straight for dessert!

"Truly I tell you, unless you change and become like children, you will never enter the kingdom of heaven."

Matthew 18:3

> ### All I Want

All I want is someone who will accept me as I am, who will challenge me to be all I am—nothing more, nothing less.

I want someone who is not afraid to tell me the truth, but who does it with love, not a bludgeon.

That's all I want.

A friend loves at all times, and kinsfolk are born to share adversity.

Proverbs 17:17

The Accident

"Your wife will make it, but we won't know the full extent of her injuries for a while."

The doctor's words reverberate in my head. In place of my wife's beautiful features are now bruises, swelling, cuts, stitches. I can handle that. It's this other, this unknown, I fear.

"Possible brain damage," the doctor said. Will she still be the woman I married when she comes out of this? How will her personality have changed? Will we have to get to know each other all over? Will she remember me?

Will she still love me?

Therefore, beloved, while you are waiting
for these things, strive to be found by him at
peace, without spot or blemish.
                                        2 Peter 3:14

Anger or Hurt?

Which came first, the anger or the hurt? Some say that behind every deep anger lies an even deeper hurt. Others say that buried behind each hurt is unresolved anger.

Sometimes it can be easier to be angry than to acknowledge the hurt behind the anger. Sometimes it can be easier to act hurt than acknowledge the anger underlying the hurt.

Whichever came first, whichever the connection, both anger and hurt are there and need to be reckoned with.

"So have no fear of them; for nothing is covered up that will not be uncovered, and nothing secret that will not become known."
Matthew 10:26

Opposites

He's the kind that loves deadlines and the last-minute crunch to get things done under the wire. He thrives on crisis. It stirs him to greater creativity, a rush of excitement.

She's the kind that hates deadlines. Her work is always done ahead of time, so that when the deadline comes she can sit back and smugly sip a cup of coffee while others rush around. She prefers to work at her own pace, creating her own schedule.

Sometimes they complement each other.

Sometimes they drive each other crazy.

Look at all the works of the Most High;
they come in pairs, one the opposite of the
other.

Sirach 33:15

| Flame |

Like a moth drawn to flame,

I'm drawn to you;

but I'm afraid if I get too close

I will lose everything.

---

*"I came to bring fire to the earth, and how
I wish it were already kindled"*

Luke 12:49

Hot, Hot...Cold!

Some of our games I like to play, but not this one.

We won't tell the other person what we really want but instead make each other guess what we have in mind. We give little hints ("You're hot, you're hot...you're cold!"), but we never let the other win.

Let's put this game in the trash bin...where it belongs.

Some friends play at friendship but a true friend sticks closer than one's nearest kin.
Proverbs 18:24

Consideration

He got upset the other day because I made plans for a friend of one of our children to stay over and I didn't clear it with him first.

So when a neighbor called today to ask if her kids could spend some time at our place—when I have to work and he is home—I called him to see if that would be all right.

I just can't help wondering whether he will consider my feelings the next time he makes plans when my time is involved.

———————————

Husbands, in the same way, show consider-
ation for your wives in your life together.
                                              1 Peter 3:7

Leap of Faith

Marriage is a leap of faith.

That's leap, as in "to dive into or jump off of or over...."

And faith, as in "to believe, without certainty or proof."

Indeed, you are my lamp, O Lord, the Lord lightens my darkness. By you I can crush a troop, and by my God I can leap over a wall.

2 Samuel 22:30

Butterfly

We are struggling in this cocoon of our marriage. What was once warm and cozy, safe and secure, now feels tight and confining. There's little room for either of us to grow.

It's time to break out. Together we can take off and enter a whole new butterfly stage.

———————————

From his fullness we have all received,
grace upon grace.

John 1:16

Magic

There was something magical about the actors and crew of the Starship Enterprise. I've heard it said that these people not only worked together but genuinely liked each other.

Sometimes in real life we find similar magic. People, ideas and circumstances come together in ways that seem magical.

But after so many years, I know it's not just magic that keeps us together. A lot of hard work goes into maintaining our marriage.

Still, a bit of magic remains in the air.

And the angel said to me, "Write this: Blessed are those who are invited to the marriage supper of the Lamb."
Revelation 19:9

The Power of Touch

Small things—a gesture, a kind word, a look, a touch—make a difference. Some days I get far away from myself, and the only way to get back is a touch from you.

You don't realize the power that resides in your hands. It is restorative, a curative for all that ails me.

Wherever (Jesus) went, into villages or cities or farms, they laid the sick in the marketplaces, and begged him that they might touch even the fringe of his cloak; and all who touched it were healed.

Mark 6:56

A Moment—Part 2

I've been away with the kids for days. We've had a great time, but we all miss you.

We can't wait to get back and tell you how much we love you. We plan to fill that awkward moment when we first arrive with pleasant smiles and hugs.

But the kids fuss and fight and make demands the whole trip back. At home, they jump out of the car and run around, almost knocking me over as I try to empty the trunk.

You come to the door, holler at the kids, and try to restore order.

Somehow, the moment is lost.

May mercy, peace, and love be yours in abundance.

Jude :2

Listen to What I Hear

Listen to what I hear,
    not what you mean.

When you storm off,
    I hear you abandoning me.

When you give me the silent treatment,
    I hear reproach.

When you make fun of or ridicule me,
    I hear that you don't respect me.

Listen to what I hear,
    not what you mean.

------

*Listen, and hear my voice; pay attention,
and hear my speech.*

                                        Isaiah 28:23

> ## Thunderstorms—Part 1

"Crack!" "Boom!"

"What are you doing?" I ask. He should be inside where it's safe, not out on the porch in a thunderstorm. When ordinary people head for cover, he heads for the porch.

"Watching the storm," he says. "It's fantastic."

I don't understand this man I married, but it's too late now. It's either stay inside where it's safe or join him in the whirlwind.

"Come on," he calls.

I jump into the fray.

His way is in whirlwind and storm, and the clouds are the dust of his feet.

Nahum 1:3

> ### Standing By

I see your hurt, but I don't know how to help you. All my best efforts seem to make things worse. I feel so helpless.

I hate to see you in pain. I hate knowing you are hurting and I can't help. But these are things only you can work out for yourself. I know you may fail miserably or you may succeed.

That's why I'm standing by.

Whatever happens, I hope you know I'm here.

Whatever happens, I hope you know I care.

Do not, therefore, abandon that confidence of yours; it brings a great reward. For you need endurance, so that when you have done the will of God, you may receive what was promised.

Hebrews 10:35-36

Mothers-in-Law

She must have talked to her mother today. I know that look. Now I'll hear all evening about her sister Suzie's husband the stock broker and all their money.

He must have talked to his mother. I can tell. There's that angry wall about him. What did she say this time? How do I find out?

Now she'll complain about the bills and our inability to take trips like Suzie.

Now he'll snap at any suggestion I make no matter how reasonable.

She must have talked to her mother....

He must have talked to his mother....

Greet his mother—a mother to me also.
Romans 16:13

Mother, May I?

Mother, may I?

No, you may not! I'm not your mother, so don't treat me as if I were. You don't have to ask permission for everything you do. Nor do I want you to sneak behind my back like a rebellious teenager seeing what you can get away with.

Those decisions that are ours to make, we'll make together. Those decisions that are yours alone, you must make yourself.

If you want my input, you've got it, but if it's not for me to decide, don't put me in that position. Neither lock me out nor give me too much power. Just let me be your friend.

Not your mother.

Whenever you face trials of any kind, consider it nothing but a joy, because you know that the testing of your faith produces endurance; and let endurance have its full effect, so that you may be mature and complete, lacking in nothing.

James 1:2-4

Opening Up

When we first started dating, you always used to say, "Talk, don't not say anything." But what is there to say, I would think, believing somehow that my thoughts were being communicated telepathically. I was wrong.

I learned to open up. It happened slowly. I came to realize I'm not the center of the universe and that everyone and everything are not focused on me. I learned that I had to make an effort to communicate. You taught me well.

After all these years, though, I still have to remind myself of this, because my inclination is still to assume that you know what I'm thinking.

"Do not be afraid, but speak and do not be silent; for I am with you, and no one will lay a hand on you to harm you."
Acts 18:9-10

Ghosts

Our parents haunt our relationship.

Their relationships affect ours in hundreds of ways—slipping through the cracks, prying us apart, pushing us over the edge. They are in our bed at night. They follow us during the day. They provoke our arguments and anger.

Lord, we need to let them go.

"I will follow you, Lord; but let me first say farewell to those at my home."

Luke 9:61

The Harder Task

Women are asked to submit to their husbands; men are asked to love their wives.

Which is the harder of the two tasks?

_____

Wives, be subject to your husbands as you are to the Lord....Husbands, love your wives, just as Christ loved the church and gave himself up for her.
                                        Ephesians 5:22, 25

Love—Part 3

For all that we are enamored of the word "love" in our society— I love chocolate, I love that movie, I love my kids, I love my job—we have only one term to express this multifaceted reality.

So when I say, "I love you," the word is completely inadequate in expressing how I feel for you—my partner, my best friend, my spouse, my lover.

Little children, let us love, not in word or speech, but in truth and action.

1 John 3:18

> ### Chipping Paint

The paint on one side of the house is badly peeling and in need of care. But the rest of the house isn't so bad. We could easily get by for another year or two.

Do we put up siding, removing the need to ever paint again but leaving us with a big debt?

Do we just paint the one side, chipping away at the layers that need to be removed so that we can apply fresh paint?

Or do we paint the whole house, even that part not needing it?

Our marriage is like our house: We've got lots of options, but we've got to keep it up.

Let the favor of the Lord our God be upon us, and prosper for us the work of our hands—O prosper the work of our hands!
Psalm 90:17

Power

You know me better than anyone else. You know my weaknesses, where I am most vulnerable. You know how to hurt me as no one else can. I gave you that power over me when we married. So please be careful what you say and do.

For this very reason, you must make every effort to support your faith with goodness, and goodness with knowledge, and knowl-edge with self-control, and self-control with endurance, and endurance with godliness, and godliness with mutual affection, and mutual affection with love.

2 Peter 1:5-7

Self-Esteem

More marriages are lost to low self-esteem than to any other cause.

How can I help build my partner's self-esteem today?

What words or actions can I use to say "I love you" and "You are important"?

My child, honor yourself with humility, and give yourself the esteem you deserve.
                                        Sirach 10:28

Fascination...and Fear

Women fascinate me. What is it about them? The way they look and act and smell and talk—so different from men. There is something animalistic about them, and I'm sure that is part of their attraction.

Women also scare me a little bit. They don't fight like men, who strut like roosters and beg to prove who's on top. Women are much more likely to use words—carefully chosen, well-placed, stinging.

Yes, women are different from men, but it's sure interesting having them around—especially the specific one I'm married to!

The LORD has created a new thing on the earth; a woman encompasses a man.
Jeremiah 31:22

Beauty and the Beast

It's an old myth that if we love someone long and hard enough, they will change. Love can transform even a beast into a handsome prince. Love conquers all.

But if we truly love someone, we accept that person—beast and all—without hiding a secret agenda to transform him or her into someone or something else.

I will accept you, says the Lord GOD.
Ezechiel 43:27

Second Best

I can handle secondhand clothes, secondhand furniture, floor models with nicks and dents. I don't need a lot of money or things to be happy, to feel good about myself and my life.

I can handle second best when it comes to the things in our life.

I can't accept second best when it comes to your love.

Oh, may your breasts be like clusters of the vine, and the scent of your breath like apples, and your kisses like the best wine that goes down smoothly, gliding over lips and teeth.

Song of Songs 7:8-9

| Independence Day |

This is the day I declare my independence
    from your overarching demands,
    from your taxing nature,
    from your idiosyncracies,
    from your impertinence,
    from your choice of toothpaste.

Now I declare my dependence
    on your wonderful sense of humor,
    on your sensitivity during times of stress,
    on your funny little expressions,
    on your way with people and children,
    on your choice of cologne.

---

*In the Lord woman is not independent of
man or man independent of woman.*
                    1 Corinthians 11:11

Aching Feet

The little boy wakes up. It's dark. It must be late. He creeps down the stairs, half asleep.

His parents are in the kitchen, and the boy peeks around the corner and watches them.

His mom sits at the table, her feet in his dad's lap. He is rubbing them gently. They are talking and laughing together.

There is a warmth in the kitchen that makes the boy feel safe and secure. He sneaks back up the stairs.

"May the LORD reward you for your deeds, and may you have a full reward from the LORD, the God of Israel, under whose wings you have come for refuge!"

Ruth 2:12

> Resentments

I've a laundry list of resentments a mile long against you. Resentments that I've accumulated over the years—the times you failed to wake up in the middle of the night to care for crying babies, the times you forgot important dates, the times you failed to give me the help I needed with my career.

But I know resentments are deadly. They suck the life out of a marriage until nothing is left but a hollow shell.

And so I forgive you and let go of all my resentments. Just as I hope you let go of yours.

Rid yourselves, therefore, of all malice, and
all guile, insincerity, envy, and all slander.
1 Peter 2:1

Trust—Part 1

I trust you. I trust that you care for me. I trust that you want only what's best for me, that you place my well-being before your own, that you won't knowingly let me down or hurt me, that you'll catch me if I fall and help me back up again.

I trust that when you said forever, you meant it.

———————————————

I am not ashamed, for I know the one in whom I have put my trust.

           2 Timothy 1:12

> Women's Lib

My wife is in favor of women's liberation. Sometimes I hear her talk as if she feels men poison everything we touch.

But I know she loves me and I am trying to understand what she is saying.

All I know is that I never want to hurt her and I always want to do my fair share. Isn't that what marriage is all about?

———————————————

Therefore I prayed, and understanding was given me; I called on God, and the spirit of wisdom came to me.

Wisdom 7:7

Jokes

The day you brought home the nose, I laughed so hard I thought I would pull a muscle in my stomach. The nose, like mine, is huge, but this one sits on the night table as a holder for my eyeglasses.

Whenever you're out and see something funny like the nose, you pick it up for me.

God, help me to remember that jokes and surprises are fun and bring joy and laughter to a marriage.

———————————————

Then our mouth was filled with laughter,
and our tongue with shouts of joy.
                                        Psalm 122:2

> ## An Example

Our daughter is marrying. How little she knows of what lies ahead. How little she knows about the reality of married life, the good times and the bad. Can she really say "for better or worse"? Can she really say "forever"?

She walks down the aisle with her dad, my husband. I realize that our entire marriage has been one long example for her.

For better *and* for worse.

"For I have set you an example, that you also should do as I have done to you."
                                   John 13:15

Little Reminders

Getting squirted by ice-cold water when I turn on the shower because the last person to use it hadn't adjusted the faucet back to the tub.

Plugging in the vacuum cleaner and having it leap into action because it had been turned off by pulling out the plug rather than touching the off switch.

Discovering the dishwasher is full of dirty dishes and someone didn't take the time to turn it on.

Looking everywhere for the TV remote and finally finding it in the recycling bin.

Reading the Sunday newspaper and coming across a big hole where an article or an ad has been ripped out.

Irritating, but lovable, little reminders that we are, indeed, married.

Therefore I intend to keep on reminding you of these things, though you know them already.

2 Peter 1:12

Spousal Vacations

We all need vacations from our responsibilities. We need vacations from our work, breaks from our kids and the responsibilities of home life, and time off from our spouses.

Everybody is hard to live with at times. There are no perfect spouses or perfect marriages out there, so give yourself a break. Take a vacation alone for one hour or one day or longer.

Your time together will be all the sweeter for it.

Where has your beloved gone, O fairest among women? Which way has your beloved turned that we may seek him with you?

Song of Songs 6:1

| Thunderstorms—Part 2 |

Sometimes there's nothing like a good thunderstorm to clear the air and leave the earth sparkling and fresh. Other times a thunderstorm just leaves us with worse humidity, stickiness and tension in the air.

Sometimes a good fight between spouses clears the air. Sometimes it only makes matters worse.

———————————

"I will stretch out my hands to the LORD; the thunder will cease, and there will be no more hail, so that you may know that the earth is the LORD's."

Exodus 9:29

Glad

When I married you, I got a whole new family—
your parents, your siblings and their children, your
aunts and uncles, your cousins, even your friends.

Maybe I should have checked them all out more
carefully, but I didn't and I'm glad.

I'm glad because maybe if I had known them
better I would have hesitated to marry the whole bunch
of you, and what a mistake that would have been!

When I considered these things inwardly,
and pondered in my heart that in kinship
with wisdom there is immortality, and in
friendship with her, pure delight, and in the
labor of her hands, unfailing wealth, and in
the experience of her company, understand-
ing, and renown in sharing her words, I
went about seeking how to get her for
myself.

Wisdom 8:17-18

> *Sealed in Time*

One day they stopped and, if only for a moment, rediscovered the person they had married.

It happened in the kitchen while she was making phone calls to bill collectors and he was getting a drink from the refrigerator. They looked deeply into each other's eyes.

"Where did the time go?" the silence said. "How have you been?"

Without words, he put down his drink and she put down the telephone. He pulled up one of the kitchen chairs and she sat on his lap. Her head came to rest on his shoulder. He wrapped an arm around her.

"I love you."

"I love you, too."

The moment was sealed in time.

"Come, therefore, let us enjoy the good things that exist, and make use of the creation to the full as in youth."

Wisdom 2:6

Clutter—Part 1

Clutter, clutter everywhere: towels on the bathroom floor, newspapers stacked in corners, unread magazines piled on end tables, a display of children's art on the kitchen counter.

Clutter, clutter everywhere: unfinished craft projects, correspondence unanswered, stacks of unfinished novels next to the bed.

Clutter, clutter everywhere. It's not that we're proud of it, but we're not ashamed either. Some call it clutter; we call it the overflow from life.

"I came that they may have life, and have it abundantly."

John 10:10

Free Spirit

I used to be a free spirit, flitting from one thing to the next. Then you came into my life, then the kids.

You want me to be a free spirit still, to take wing on flights of fantasy. But somewhere along the line I put down roots and I no longer know how to fly.

But there's still a free spirit lurking inside me.

Will you help to set it free?

Stretch out your hand from on high; set me free and rescue me.

Psalm 144:7

Inside Looking Out

It was different when I was on the outside looking in. Marriage looked very different before we were wed. The only close look I had gotten until then was what I saw of my parents' relationship. But even that was from the outside looking in.

I didn't think it would look this way from the inside looking out.

The man looked up and said, "I can see people, but they look like trees, walking." Then Jesus laid his hands on his eyes again; and he looked intently and his sight was restored, and he saw everything clearly.

Mark 8:24-25

A Moment—Part 3

It only takes a moment to repair a breach in our relationship. A kind word or thoughtful gesture—saying "Thank you" or "I'm sorry" and really meaning it, bringing the other a cup of coffee or a pillow without being asked.

It only takes a moment to remind ourselves that we still love each other despite our differences, despite our disagreements, despite our failings and faults.

But how critical that moment can be.

———————————

You know what time it is, how it is now the moment for you to wake from sleep. For salvation is nearer to us now than when we became believers; the night is far gone, the day is near. Let us then lay aside the works of darkness and put on the armor of light.
                              Romans 13:11-12

Know Better

She should know better. When he gets that tired look, overwhelmed with life and very vulnerable, the tired look of the hard working man, the tired look of the overworked father, the tired look of the well-meaning husband; when he gets that look, it sets off something inside her. She wants him.

When, lost in his tiredness, he sits at the table, trying to be a good sport in the game of their busy life, she should know better, but she can't resist the urge to rub his shoulder and whisper sweet, seductive nothings in his ear.

Many have been seduced by a woman's beauty, and by it passion is kindled like a fire.

Sirach 9:8

Home

Wherever I go, I carry you with me. Memories we have shared. Words. Private jokes that are only between us.

I am a different person for having known you. You have changed me. You have become part of me. I am part of you.

You are the place where I find shelter and rest. Wherever I go, you are my home.

"Abide in me and I abide in you. Just as the branch cannot bear fruit by itself unless it abides in the vine, neither can you unless you abide in me."

John 15:4

Prince Charming

I sit on my porch swing on a hot summer day—
my day off—reading romance novels and fantasizing.

Then you come home, tired from the day. You are
grouchy and out-of-sorts, but you sit and talk with me
for a while before we both go in to eat.

For all your occasional lack of charm, you are my
Prince Charming.

What is your beloved more than another
beloved, O fairest among women?
Song of Songs 5:9

Commitment

Friends. She has a few. Different ones from mine and, yes, there are men among them. I imagine she would be a good friend to a man. She has good qualities—she listens well, isn't afraid to challenge shoddy thinking, shares what's going on in her life.

Once I would have been frightened by any man but me being the center of her attention—even for a short time. But we're not just friends anymore—we are husband and wife, wife and husband, spouses.

There's so much peace and freedom to be found in commitment.

You are indeed my rock and my fortress; for your name's sake lead me and guide me, take me out of the net that is hidden for me, for you are my refuge. Into your hand I commit my spirit.

Psalm 31:3-5

Money—Part 1

For the longest time, I thought money was the root of all good, the key to our making a happy life together.

But now I realize that it isn't so much the money we have as it is the things we have been through together that make the difference in the quality of our life.

Don't mistake my sentiment: Money has allowed us to do many things we might never have been able to do, but the key was being together.

Money may not be the root of all evil, but it is not the root of all good.

"Store up for yourselves treasures in heaven, where neither moth nor rust consumes and where thieves do not break in and steal. For where your treasure is, there your heart will be also."
Matthew 6:20-21

Thoroughbreds

A married couple can be like a team of fine thoroughbreds pulling together in unison. They know when to start and when to stop; when to turn to the right, when to the left; when to pick up speed, when to slow down—all in response to the driver's command.

The driver can be neither the husband nor the wife, however. The driver must be the Spirit of God.

_____

For those who live according to the flesh
set their minds on the things of the flesh,
but those who live according to the Spirit
set their minds on the things of the Spirit.
                              Romans 8:5

Hummingbirds

A hummingbird swoops about my bird feeder. As if suspended in space, he hangs in place, his little wings flapping furiously to maintain his position.

Sometimes I feel we are like that hummingbird. It takes an awful lot of energy just to stay in place.

For this I toil and struggle with all the energy that he powerfully inspires within me.

Colossians 1:29

Family Picnic

"Family Picnic" is an oxymoron. Children fight, dogs run under foot. Cousin Nell argues with Aunt Gertrude, and Uncle Charlie guzzles too much beer while he tends to the charcoal. I spent the previous afternoon cutting potatoes and vegetables for a potato salad that the children will pick apart and eventually leave uneaten on the plate. Our evening will be spent cleaning up.

We look at each other and both silently vow: Next time we eliminate either the family or the picnic.

These are blemishes on your love-feasts.
Jude :12

The Beach

We sit and watch the bodies at the beach—baby bodies, boy bodies, girl bodies, old bodies, young bodies, male and female bodies. They are all there.

It's not like in the movies or on TV. There's no Beach Blanket Bingo or Baywatch here, but real people with bumps and lumps, bellies bulging out of their swimsuits.

Then we look at our bodies—a little worse for wear, perhaps, but still attractive and exciting to each other.

Love may not be blind, but it certainly does wear rose-colored glasses!

O my dove, in the clefts of the rock, in the covert of the cliff, let me see your face, let me hear your voice; for your voice is sweet, and your face is lovely.

Song of Songs 2:14

It's too darn hot. Humidity drips thick in the air. The fan ineffectively stirs the stale, heavy air.

We lie with nothing covering us, trying to catch a breeze. We lie as far from each other as possible to avoid the heat of our bodies.

We reach out to each other and fall asleep, finger lightly touching finger.

It's just a different way to make love.

———————————————

Then a hand touched me and roused me.
                                        Daniel 10:10

Broken Trust

It wasn't supposed to be that way. I never meant to hurt you, but I did. You never meant to hurt me, but you did.

We were supposed to be there for each other, but we weren't.

Dare we trust again?

———————————————

Even my bosom friend in whom I trusted, who ate of my bread, has lifted the heel against me.

Psalm 41:9

Keep Trying—Part 1

I don't know if I'm making my point, and it's frustrating. So I say so. "Does what I'm saying mean anything to you?"

"No," she admits. "I don't understand."

So many years together and I still can't get through.

"But," she says, "I am willing to listen until I do. Are you willing to keep trying?"

Yes, I am.

Better is the end of a thing than its beginning; the patient in spirit are better than the proud in spirit.

Ecclesiastes 7:8

Charming

I sometimes forget

how charming you are,

until I see you with others.

You are direct, yet thoughtful;

strong, yet compassionate;

dynamic, yet patient.

How lucky I am

to be the main recipient

of your charm.

---

*Do not dismiss a wise and good wife, for
her charm is worth more than gold.*

Sirach 7:19

Family Vacation

The sounds of bickering and arguing come from the backseat of the car. The kids are away from their familiar haunts, friends, schedule and rules. They are completely dependent on their siblings for playmates—which spells disaster. They feel it is their obligation to test every limit we had painstakingly established on the home front.

Exhausted, we collapse on the bed at the motel. Day one of our family vacation. Will we survive? Will our marriage survive?

We look at each other and ask, "Whose idea was this anyway?"

———————————————

When I looked for good, evil came; and
when I waited for light, darkness came.
                                        Job 30:26

Work, Work, Work

Work, work, work, everything is work. I work at my job. I work on the house. I work at raising the kids. I work at prayer. I work at our relationship. I'm even supposed to work at sex.

Sometimes it seems there's just no fun anymore.

My child, do not busy yourself with many matters; if you multiply activities, you will not be held blameless. If you pursue, you will not overtake, and by fleeing you will not escape. There are those who work and struggle and hurry, but are so much the more in want.

Sirach 11:10-11

Bad Mood

I'm in a good place today. She's not. She told me so. And then she apologized and I told her that her mood is really not affecting me.

My words aren't mean. They are absolutely the truth. It's a reality I can live with—she's in a bad mood, I'm in a good one.

Now let's see what happens the next time she is in a good place...and I'm not.

―――――――――――――

The point is this: the one who sows sparingly will also reap sparingly, and the one who sows bountifully will also reap bountifully.
                    2 Corinthians 9:6

He comes home tired and hungry from a long day at work. I can see the tiredness in his body. He has yet to negotiate the change from office to home. I think: Give him some space, some breathing room.

But he and our son go at it over something that appears insignificant to me. There is yelling, anger, tears held back....

Then he stops, takes a deep breath, pauses for a moment. The two of them talk and hug, and I think: I'm so proud of my husband.

I often boast about you; I have great pride in you.

2 Corinthians 7:4

Stillborn

Together they labored to bring forth a child. He held her hand and breathed with her in her pain. But all their efforts were in vain. The baby was stillborn. What was to be their child was still theirs, but not to love and raise together...only to bury and to mourn.

_____

How long must I bear pain in my soul, and
have sorrow in my heart all day long?
                                    Psalm 13:2

A Couple—Part 1

Being a couple means you take one from two and get less than one; you put one and one together and you get more than two.

Speaking the truth in love, we must grow up in every way into him who is the head, into Christ, from whom the whole body, joined and knit together by every ligament with which it is equipped, as each part is working properly, promotes the body's growth in building itself up in love.
Ephesians 4:15-16

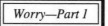

Worry—Part 1

The tornado sirens sound. I hustle the children downstairs. My thoughts turn to my husband. Where is he in this storm? Is he safe and secure, or is he out in the midst of it, responding to some emergency? I think I know the answer.

He calls later to check on our safety. I assure him that we are fine, just as I assured my children while reading to them by the dim basement light. He's remaining on call, waiting to help again should he be needed.

I'm not worried for us. My worry is for him.

Do not worry about anything, but in everything by prayer and supplication with thanksgiving let your requests be made known to God.

Philippians 4:6

Stand Back

We both need to stand back at times and look at our lives—where we have been, where we are going.

Once we've gained perspective, then we can make our decisions freely and wisely. We can choose for love—wherever that may take us.

---

*"Let us choose what is right; let us
determine among ourselves what is good."*
                                        Job 34:4

Games People Play

The games people play: breaking up and making up; being hurt and hurting back; pretending it doesn't hurt; pretending they don't care; trying to control through overt power; trying to control through covert manipulation.

I don't want to play those games—especially with you.

It is the same way with lifeless instruments that produce sound, such as the flute and the harp. If they do not give distinct notes, how will anyone know what is being played?

1 Corinthians 14:7

A Blessing

The anniversary cards to each other have become more elaborate and their handwritten notes—mighty scrawls if ever there were any—grow larger, bolder, more straightforward: "I don't know what would have happened to me without you." "Without you I would have been a bum." "You are my sunshine." "I love you."

It wasn't always like that. There were times they wouldn't even note their anniversary. But now, as they grow older, they recognize the blessing they have been to each other, and nothing will prevent them from celebrating it.

Because your steadfast love is better than life, my lips will praise you. So I will bless you as long as I live; I will lift up my hands and praise you.

Psalm 63:3-4

Dream House

It is a dream, but she persists in it anyway. The house is just around the corner—all eleven rooms of it. In her mind, each room has its use and is already decorated to perfection. If he didn't know better, he'd think they'd already moved in.

So he goes along and gets caught up in the fantasy, and pretty soon they are laughing together as if the house were theirs. Their kids call them weird, but they laugh too. It brings the whole family closer together.

Every so often, though, he wonders what will happen when the house is finally sold. But he has to stop himself: How can they lose something that they never had in the first place?

Or can they?

They shall build houses and inhabit them;
they shall plant vineyards and eat their
fruit.

Isaiah 65:21

Reacquainted

Hello, stranger, don't I remember you from somewhere? Seems we've met in passing—like two ships in the night.

Howdy, stranger, seems I know you, but I'm not sure how. Did we meet in another life, you and I?

We've shared this house, our bed, the raising of our children. But now that the kids are gone, it seems I hardly know you.

Maybe it's time we got reacquainted.

I was overjoyed to find some of your children walking in the truth, just as we have been commanded by the Father. But now, dear lady, I ask you, not as though I were writing you a new commandment, but one we have had from the beginning, let us love one another.

2 John :4-5

The perfect age:

    to be young enough

    that sex is still passionate,

    yet old enough

    that it has become tender.

---

*I passed by you again and looked on you;
you were the age for love.*

                Ezechiel 16:8

Real intimacy is never easy, especially in this hurry-up, never-enough-time culture of ours.

Intimacy, like trust, requires time to develop. It is the result of experience, not intention.

I'll make time for it if you'll make time for it.

Day by day, as they spent much time together in the temple, they broke bread at home and ate their food with glad and generous hearts.

Acts 2:46

Competition

Like a rabbit I dart ahead. My brain goes a mile a minute, flitting here and there from one idea to another. There appears to be no logic to my madness.

I plod along, bit by bit. Consistency, I say. Balance. Just keep at it every day. I work things out in a logical fashion and then proceed. Slow and steady wins the race.

"Who's racing?"

Let us not become conceited, competing against one another, envying one another.
                    Galatians 5:26

Resentful

Part of marriage is giving up. Compromising. Not always getting your way.

But I didn't realize that marriage would also mean letting you do certain things that I would no longer do, and that in giving those up I would eventually lose part of my ability to do them myself. You take care of the car, so I no longer know how to do it myself. You do most of the cooking, so I'm forgetting all my little secrets for making the perfect soufflé.

It's a small thing, really a tiny thing. And in its place I gain so much.

Still, it's funny how I resent it.

———————————

The king of Israel set out toward home,
resentful and sullen.

1 Kings 20:43

Compromise—Part 2

Two kids were enough. Two were manageable. At least that is how she felt before the third one came along unexpectedly.

He didn't really have a problem with a big family. He came from one. Three, four, five kids—what's the difference? "After the third one you might as well have ten," he would laugh and say.

She didn't think it was all that funny, and they compromised on four.

It was the right number...for them.

---

*I appointed you to go and bear fruit, fruit
that will last, so that the Father will give
you whatever you ask him in my name.*
                                        John 15:16

Worry—Part 2

When you are late, I get worried. Where does my anxiety come from? I know you're responsible; I know you're trustworthy; I know you're busy. But the world is filled with dangerous situations. Accidents happen every day. You never know when something bad might happen. I wish you would call. It would make things so much easier.

I would take the time to call if I could. But you know you can trust me; you know I'm responsible; you know I'm busy. Yes, the world is filled with dangerous situations and accidents do happen every day. But nothing bad is going to happen. I wish I could call, but I will be home soon.

"You are worried and distracted by many things; there is need of only one thing."
                    Luke 10:41-42

Body Rhythms

My body rhythms are so often out of sync with your body rhythms.

When you're up, I'm down.

When you're down, I'm up.

When you want fun, I'm ready to work.

When I want mindless recreation, you want meaningful dialogue.

Our body rhythms are often out of sync, but when they do meet....

Watch out!

For the elements changed places with one another, as on a harp the notes vary the nature of the rhythm, while each note remains the same.

Wisdom 19:18

Salad

People say we are like two peas in a pod.

They miss the point. It's not that we are alike; it's that we are happy together.

If people could see that we are really more like apples and oranges or kiwi and pineapple than anything else, then they might understand.

What makes us special is that we are like a salad....

With complementary ingredients that explode on the palate.

Your channel is an orchard of pomegranates with all the choicest fruits, henna with nard, nard and saffron, calamus and cinnamon, with all the trees of frankincense, myrrh and aloes, with all chief spices.

Song of Songs 4:13-14

Happy

First it was a matter of looking around to see who seemed happy.

Then it became a matter of envying those I thought were happy.

Next it was a matter of realizing that I am happy myself.

Now it is a matter of being happy knowing that I am happy with another—and that another is happy with me.

(Wisdom) is a tree of life to those who lay hold of her; those who hold her fast are called happy.

Proverbs 3:18

I'm afraid that if I can't

    analyze

        rescue

            save

                control

                    you

I'll have to

    analyze

        rescue

            save

                control

                    myself.

There is no fear in love, but perfect love
casts out fear; for fear has to do with
punishment, and whoever fears has not
reached perfection in love.

                        1 John 4:18

Hurt

I want to hurt the people who hurt you. I want it so bad I can almost taste their blood in my mouth.

I want to hurt the people who hurt you. They have taken from you something so precious, and they have taken something precious from me.

If only it had been me they had hurt.

For the hurt of my poor people I am hurt, I mourn, and dismay has taken hold of me.
Jeremiah 8:21

Getting Through

We can get through this. That's what I keep telling myself. If I just hold on long enough we'll get through the worst. There will be good times again.

Sometimes I want to bail out. Seeing you in so much pain for so long. Knowing you are not able to respond to me in the way I want, in the way I need. Then I feel so selfish.

We can get through this, I keep telling myself. If we can just hang in there. Just around the corner is the promise of a bright new relationship, better than before.

If we can just get through this.

"Very truly, I tell you, you will weep and mourn, but the world will rejoice; you will have pain, but your pain will turn into joy."
John 16:20

> *Pinching Pennies*

Take care of the pennies and the dollars will take care of themselves, my dad always said.

If I hear one more of your dad's sayings I'm going to scream. I hate feeling pinched for pennies, like we can't afford to buy a magazine or go to a movie if we want.

But what does it hurt to go without something now and then? With the money saved over the long term we could buy something we've always wanted.

Fine, I'll treat us to lunch!

That's *not* what I meant!

———————————

If you love to listen you will gain knowledge, and if you pay attention you will become wise.

Sirach 6:33

> *The Cold War*

They take cheap shots at each other at parties and family gatherings. Jokes that aren't funny to anyone. The bitterness is so thick it threatens to obliterate anyone caught in the cross fire. Where once there was passion, there is now only the bitterness of years of disappointments and unexpressed, swallowed anger, frozen in time.

They stayed together for their children, but their children are being frozen by their war.

"From whose womb did the ice come forth, and who has given birth to the hoarfrost of heaven?"

Job 38:29

They say, take care of your man and he'll take care of you. Anticipate his every need, even before he has one.

They say, bring her flowers and treat her like the princess she is. Don't worry her with troubles at work or financial concerns.

They say....

But we say no.

A fool takes no pleasure in understanding, but only in expressing personal opinion.
Proverbs 18:2

The Affairs

The "other woman" wasn't a woman; it was his job. The "other man" wasn't a man; it was her kids. They looked elsewhere for what was lacking in their marriage.

———————————————

Whoever digs a pit will fall into it, and a stone will come back on the one who starts it rolling.

Proverbs 26:27

His, Hers and Theirs

He brought his children into the marriage, she brought hers. It was a wedding of two separate and functioning families with established patterns of how to do things, ways of communicating, ways of not communicating.

Is there any wonder they clashed so hard?

And yet somehow, they have managed to build a new life together where others have failed.

What was once his family and her family has become their family.

For this reason I bow my knees before the Father, from whom every family in heaven and on earth takes its name.
                                    Ephesians 3:14-15

The Source

What it is they cannot name, but it causes many sensations: desire, longing, passion, trust, faith, good will, caring, forgiveness—yes, even the capacity to take risks.

How could they experience something so wonderful, multifaceted, multilayered, various and mutable?

It is a sheer mystery to them, but they know its source.

"I am the Alpha and the Omega, the beginning and the end. To the thirsty I will give water as a gift from the spring of the water of life."

Revelation 21:6

Duet

male female

female   male

in a dance of life

                in a dance of love

sometimes high

                sometimes low

alto   tenor

mixed with color

                shaded with gray

tinged with sadness

                filled with expectation

soprano   bass

separate   together

in-love   out-of-love

together   separate

in the mystery of the dance

Let them praise his name with dancing,
making melody to him with tambourine and
lyre.

                                        Psalm 149:3

If We Only Knew

If we only knew what lie ahead of us, would we have the strength to go on?

If we knew the pain, the hurt, the disillusionment?

If we knew the joy beyond the pain, the laughter through the tears, the love amidst the sorrows of life?

If we only knew.

But we don't.

And so we choose to go forward.

Surely there is a future, and your hope will not be cut off.

Proverbs 23:18

Tending to the Roots

Sometimes our plants grow wild and long. Vines grow and stretch to the floor, leaving that which is closest to the pot bare and lifeless. All of the plants' energies go into producing new shoots far away from the roots.

But eventually the burden of supporting these long growths proves too much, and the new shoots die as whole branches wither. So periodically we trim back our plants to encourage fuller growth, closer to the roots.

In the same way we have to trim back our activities at times in order to tend to those that are most important.

_____

"I am the true vine, and my Father is the vinegrower. He removes every branch in me that bears no fruit. Every branch that bears fruit he prunes to make it bear more fruit."

John 15:1-3

> *A Mystery—Part 1*

Ask us how we have stayed together for as long as we have, and it makes perfect sense to us—although it is a mystery.

The longer we stay together, the mystery just grows deeper—although it still makes perfect sense!

The mystery...has been hidden throughout the ages and generations but has now been revealed to his saints.

Colossians 1:26

Surprises

You keep surprising me.

Sometimes pleasantly.

Sometimes not so pleasantly.

But at least you're not predictable.

When you did awesome deeds that we did not expect, you came down, the mountains quaked at your presence.

Isaiah 64:3

> *Unfettered*

When I was a child, I couldn't wait to be on my own so I could do what I wanted, whenever I wanted.

But I'd rather be held back by you than go on unfettered but alone.

Turn to me and be gracious to me, for I am lonely.

Psalm 26:16

To Yell or Not to Yell

He likes being the nice guy. He grew up in a home where yelling was the norm, and he vowed that nobody in his household would have to make a scene to be heard.

She, on the other hand, grew up in a home where nobody as much as raised a voice. She wants everyone in the family to be noticed, and she is not afraid of a little yelling.

So she yells and he doesn't, and their children do a little bit of both. Together, they've developed a family system that works for them.

The Lord is merciful and gracious, slow to anger and abiding in steadfast love. He will not always accuse, nor will he keep his anger forever.

                              Psalm 103:8-9

> ## The Best Medicine

I love to laugh.

Every time I see Ed Wynn as Uncle Albert in the movie *Mary Poppins*—which isn't all that often now that the kids are grown—I feel my spirits rise. I might as well join the bunch of them having tea on the ceiling.

So when I laugh, don't take it personally. Like Uncle Albert, I literally can't help myself!

The LORD said to Abraham, "Why did Sarah laugh, and say, 'Shall I indeed bear a child, now that I am old?' Is anything too wonderful for the LORD? At the set time I will return to you, in due season, and Sarah shall have a son." But Sarah denied, saying, "I did not laugh"; for she was afraid. He said, "Oh yes, you did laugh."
> *Genesis 18:13-15*

Collision Course—Part 2

I can't wait to retire in a few more years. After so many years of nine-to-five drudgery, I want to be able to schedule my own time, to stay at home with my loved ones, and to read books before a roaring fire.

With all of the kids finally out on their own, I can finally do some things for myself: go back to school, focus on a second career. I look forward to anything that will get me back into society.

I can't wait to stay home.

I can't wait to get out.

———————————

I wish that all were as I myself am. But each has a particular gift from God, one having one kind and another a different kind.

1 Corinthians 7:7

> *Rebirth*

The marriage they had is over. Time for them to let go of the past and move on.

But somehow, out of the rubble and the charred wood, new life is beginning to form.

The old had to end in order for the new to begin.

I consider that the sufferings of this present time are not worth comparing with the glory about to be revealed to us.
                              Romans 8:18

Fool

She thought that he was leaving his wife for her. Even though it had never been stated, that was her hope, her expectation, her tacit understanding.

She was a fool. Men don't leave their wives for the other woman. They leave their wives for themselves.

———————————

Weep for the dead, for he has left the light behind; and weep for the fool, for he has left intelligence behind. Weep less bitterly for the dead, for he is at rest; but the life of the fool is worse than death.

Sirach 22:11

Demands

Our children's demands on my time and energy are insatiable. I am the wonder-worker with the magic wand capable of granting their every wish. I am also the wicked old witch withholding what is rightfully theirs just on my whim. I am expected to fill their days with fun and entertainment, and the minute I lose my cool it's my fault, not theirs.

Sometimes I feel as if you are making yet more demands on my limited time and energy and, when there isn't enough to go around, once again I am to blame.

Remember my chains. Grace be with you.
Colossians 4:18

Sometimes I feel as if I give you my worst. My best goes to the kids and my job. The kids expect one hundred percent. The boss demands one hundred and ten percent. You get what's left over at the end of the day.

But a marriage can't survive on a diet of leftovers. I'm making you a seven-course dinner tonight!

When they were satisfied, he told his disciples, "Gather up the fragments left over, so that nothing may be lost."
John 6:12

Busy Couple

The names of Priscilla and Aquila appear five times in the New Testament. They are one of the few married couples who are both mentioned as being leaders in the early church.

Unfortunately, we know little of their relationship or their shared ministry, or they might have become an example and role model for all Christian marriages.

They were probably too busy balancing their work, family and community responsibilities to take the time to boast about themselves.

(Apollos) began to speak boldly in the synagogue, but when Priscilla and Aquila heard him, they took him aside and explained the Way of God more accurately to him.

Acts 18:26

Don't you see I have to take advantage of this opportunity now? I may never have it again. If I don't strike while the coals are hot I may lose the opportunity forever. My career will go down the tubes and with it our financial security.

I know sometimes I neglect you for the kids. But don't you see they are only young once? We have only this short time when they are young that they really need us and want us to be around. There will be plenty of time for us when the kids are grown and gone.

This golden opportunity is once in a lifetime.

Our kids are only young once.

For I handed on to you as of first impor-
tance what I had in turn received.
1 Corinthians 15:3

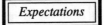

Expectations

We place so many demands on marriage today. Needs that once were filled by extended family, friends, neighbors, and even churches are now the almost exclusive concern of this one small relationship.

There's no one to help with the childrearing or finances, spouses are expected to be each other's best friend, employers force families to move often and far, even religious education and spirituality have been made primarily the responsibility of the couple.

No wonder so many marriages are cracking under the pressure.

———————————————

Their hearts were bowed down with hard labor; they fell down, with no one to help.
Psalm 107:12

Rut—Part 2

We're in a rut. We get up, sip coffee, read the morning paper, go about our respective lives.

Evenings are filled with quiet meals together. We go to the same restaurants. (Whenever we try some place new, it seems we are disappointed.)

We know our routine so well, it takes a major effort to break out of it. We hardly need to talk. We save our conversation for important matters.

After so many years together, we are in a rut. But it's a nice rut.

You shall eat in plenty and be satisfied, and praise the name of the LORD your God, who has dealt wondrously with you.

Joel 2:26

Time and Effort

A relationship takes time and effort.

Sometimes the effort is, well, effortless. Sometimes the time seems, well, timeless.

Other times the effort seems, well, not worth the effort. And the time seems, well, there just isn't any time.

Still, a relationship takes time and effort.

---

*Lead a life worthy of the calling to which
you have been called, with all humility and
gentleness, with patience, bearing with one
another in love, making every effort to
maintain the unity of the Spirit in the bond
of peace.*

Ephesians 4:1-3

A Mystery—Part 2

In the best of relationships there have to be a few hidden elements.

Even with our best and closest friend, we don't have to share everything.

There needs to be room for mystery in our marriage.

"Why are you so amazed? I will tell you the mystery of the woman, and of the beast with seven heads and ten horns that carries her."

Revelation 17:7

Disappointment

She was well into her sixties when she divorced him. While she never said much, we knew she just had too much disappointment trying to keep things together. The relationship drained her. She wanted a life, and she couldn't have it with him.

Let's make sure nobody can ever say the same about us.

For I resolved to live according to wisdom, and I was zealous for the good, and I shall never be disappointed.

Sirach 51:18

Appreciation—Part 2

We are the busy ones!

The achievers!

People appreciate us!

They wouldn't know how to get along without us!

We are so busy...

That we never take time to appreciate what others do for us.

———————————

If you do good, know to whom you do it, and you will be thanked for your good deeds.

Sirach 12:1

> *Pleasure*

What can we do to increase the pleasure we bring to each other, so that whatever pain we suffer disappears like a quick rain shower and leaves a rainbow—a banner of our love—across the sky?

My beloved speaks and says to me: "Arise, my love, my fair one, and come away; for now the winter is past, the rain is over and gone. The flowers appear on the earth; the time of singing has come, and the voice of the turtledove is heard in our land."
Song of Songs 2:10-12

> *The Grace of God*

My sister calls. She's getting a divorce. I hang up in shock. Of all the couples I know, of all the marriages, theirs appeared the most solid. Theirs was the relationship I was sure would survive all the difficult times.

I hang up and pray. Both for her and for her husband, but also for us and our own marriage.

There, but for the grace of God, go we.

"If you forgive others their trespasses, your heavenly Father will also forgive you."
Matthew 6:14

In-Laws

In-laws! Sometimes I want to shoot them. If only I lived in the Wild West. I'd track them down wearing my white hat and spurs, atop my faithful horse. I'd follow them across miles of desert, endure endless hardship in search of them. But then, unlike the good guys of old, I'd administer my own justice. I'd be judge and jury, and their punishment would be a good, old-fashioned lynching.

He treated his parents-in-law with great respect.

Tobit 14:13

It Takes Two

It takes two to tango.

And two to tangle.

Which will it be?

It was he who created humankind in the beginning, and he left them in the power of their own free choice.

Sirach 15:14

Change

It used to be that one partner in a marriage brought home the bacon and the other partner cooked it.

Now both bring home the bacon, and there's nobody around to cook it.

Rejoice insofar as you are sharing Christ's suffering, so that you may also be glad and shout for joy when his glory is revealed.

1 Peter 4:13

The Legacy

Let's imagine our own legacy.

We stand on a mountaintop, holding a single torch in our hands.

Our story is a light that shows the way for all couples who follow us.

———————————————

"You are the light of the world. A city built on a hill cannot be hid. No one after lighting a lamp puts it under the bushel basket, but on the lampstand, and it gives light to all in the house."

Matthew 5:14-15

> *Living / Staying Together*

The phrase "living together" is exciting. It even has a slightly naughty connotation—even for married couples like us. But "living together" is an accurate description of what we do.

"Staying together," on the other hand, doesn't capture the dynamics of what is really going on between us. Couples who merely "stay together" are just playing it safe, afraid to look at their relationship or take the risk of pushing it to a new level.

So, let us—you and I—continue to live together, even as we stay together.

———————————

The living, the living, they thank you, as I do this day; fathers make known to children your faithfulness. The LORD will save me, and we will sing on stringed instruments all the days of our lives, at the house of the LORD.

Isaiah 38:19-20

Something Right / Wrong

I shuffle the kids out the door to the car, hurriedly trying to pull everything together at the last minute. He gives me an angry look and growls under his breath. I wonder, what did I do wrong?

I get home from the cross-country meet, kids in tow. She gives me "the look" which says something is wrong and I should know what that something is.

I go about my daily routine and for some reason out of the blue, he kisses me. I guess I did something right.

I wash the dishes and help the kids with their homework then sit down for a few moments with the newspaper. She sneaks up behind me and plops a kiss on the top of my head. I must have done something right.

"Father, forgive them; for they do not know what they are doing."
                                        Luke 23:34

Clutter—Part 2

I have discovered a new defense in the battle against clutter: If it *can* be thrown away, it *must* be thrown away. Diligently I rip through drawers, closets, cupboards throwing out everything but the essential.

What are you doing? How could you throw this out, or that? They are treasured items, memories to be saved. Who knows when some of them might come in handy. The rule is: If it can *be saved, it* must *be saved.*

You are having the same struggle that you saw I had and now hear that I still have.
Philippians 1:30

First Kiss

I remember the first time we kissed. You were driving me to a meeting, the way you had off and on for the past year, and suddenly it was time. I don't remember your words, only your lips pressed up against mine ever so lightly.

Despite the fact that it's been years since it happened, I have never forgotten how sweet you tasted that day.

———————————————

Let him kiss me with the kisses of his mouth! For your love is better than wine.
                                        Song of Songs 1:2

> ### *Heading for the Hills*

We'll get through this, I remind myself. After all, you put up with me through all of my midlife career changes, through my motorcycle adventures and attempts to recapture my youth. I can put up with your hot flashes, hot temper, and cold shoulder.

But how long, Lord, how much longer?

Time to hop on my motorcycle and head for the hills for a while.

"Flee for your life; do not look back or stop anywhere in the Plain; flee to the hills, or else you will be consumed."

Genesis 19:17

Weddings

We cry at weddings because of the awesomeness of what the couple are undertaking. Those of us who have been married know far too well the trials that these young people are yet to discover. We have experienced the tremendous difficulty of two people making a life together, the pitfalls, the ruts, the patterns that develop, the hardships along the way.

Even those of us in happy marriages recognize that it hasn't been easy. What these young people are about to undertake is more than a vow; it is a vocation for life, with all of the struggles involved in being faithful to any vocation.

At each wedding, we relive the years of our own marriage, the bitter and the sweet. And that is why we cry.

One generation shall laud your works to another, and shall declare your mighty acts.

Psalm 145:4

Together

I am yours.

You are mine.

Together we chase away loneliness.

Together we discover what it is to love.

---

*How very good and pleasant it is when
kindred live together in unity! It is like the
precious oil on the head, running down
upon the beard, on the beard of Aaron,
running down over the collar of his robes.
It is like the dew of Hermon, which falls on
the mountains of Zion. For there the Lord
ordained his blessing, life forevermore.*
Psalm 133:1-3

Not Fair

When *his father* worked around the home or with the kids, he was paid with attention and appreciation for doing the unusual.

When *he* works around the home or with the kids, it is usual and expected...and he doesn't get paid at all.

It's just, but it's not fair.

———————————————

"The laborer deserves to be paid."
                    Luke 10:7

> *Him and Her*

Her voice brings a smile to his face. His voice tickles her soul.

Her touch arouses in him a thousand wonderful associations. His touch soothes in her the tension that builds throughout the day.

Her kiss is a balm for what ails him. His kiss is a salve for the slights she has had to suffer.

There is never too much of her for him.

There is never too much of him for her.

"From everyone to whom much has been given, much will be required; and from the one to whom much has been entrusted, even more will be demanded."

Luke 12:48

Morning and Night

Ah, the morning. The quiet of a new day. The sun rises, birds sing. My heart sings too. New beginnings, bright with promise, await me.

Ah, the evening. Sunset and starry skies. Rest after a full day of work. Quiet to sit and just be. Kids sleep. Owls hoot. My soul is at rest.

My best ideas and moods always come in the morning. I long to share this time with you.

My best ideas and moods always come at night. I long to share this time with you.

If only all days were only mornings.

If only all days were only nights.

"Where is the way to the dwelling of light, and where is the place of darkness, that you may take it to its territory and that you may discern the paths to its home?"
Job 38:19-20

Knowing Ourselves

Plato wrote, "The life which is unexamined is not worth living," and the same is true for marriage.

With all the running around we do, however, we're not very good at examining our relationship and knowing ourselves as a couple.

Still, let's keep trying.

It's worth it.

_____

You know when I sit down and when I rise up; you discern my thoughts from far away. You search out my path and my lying down and are acquainted with all my ways.
Psalm 139:2-3

"Forgive Me"

Things changed after he stopped saying only that he was sorry for upsetting her and started asking her to forgive him. It was a little step, but he worked hard to remember to say it: "Forgive me." And, after being forgiven many times, he noticed the occasions of upsetting her diminished.

That's when he realized that love and forgiveness go hand in hand.

Happy are those whose transgression is forgiven, whose sin is covered.

Psalm 32:1

> *Supportive*

You know, I thought we were in this thing for better or for worse. But as soon as I decide things aren't going well at work and would like to start thinking about going into business on my own, you balk. I can understand your wanting to keep our lifestyle as it is; I just don't understand your wanting me to kill myself over it.

I know you're sick of working where you are now. But this idea is full of holes. I don't want to see you get suckered into something that you are going to hate. I want to be supportive, but I don't want to be stupid. I know you are not happy with what you're doing, but I can't become a cheerleader if I don't think things are going to work out.

I just want you to be supportive.

I am supportive, but sometimes I can't be supportive in exactly the way you want.

> *"You made Adam, and for him you made*
> *his wife Eve as a helper and support. From*
> *the two of them the human race has sprung.*
> *You said, 'It is not good that the man*
> *should be alone; let us make a helper for*
> *him like himself.'"*
>
> *Tobit 8:6*

Mistake

For the week she was away on a business trip, he thought he did a good job organizing the household, dealing with the kids, managing schedules and meals.

And he told her so the night she got home. "I think things were a little more organized while you were away," he said.

As soon as the words were out, he knew he had made a mistake.

"Well, maybe I should have stayed away," she said in a hurt voice.

That wasn't what he meant.

All of us make many mistakes. Anyone who makes no mistakes in speaking is perfect, able to keep the whole body in check with a bridle.

James 3:2

Abuse—Part 2

They could see how it could happen to someone else. Now they see how it could happen to them.

Mental and physical abuse within marriage—it's a monster that lurks in the most unlikely places.

———————————

Have regard for your covenant, for the
dark places of the land are full of the
haunts of violence.

Psalm 74:20

Not to Us

Sometimes someone mentions that a couple we know is divorcing and we think, "How could they even consider a divorce? They've been together for years, and they seemed so happy. How? When? Why? What happened?"

And then we think, "We all have our problems, don't we?" We think, "It could happen to anyone...but not to us."

In the day of prosperity be joyful, and in the day of adversity consider: God has made the one as well as the other.

Ecclesiastes 7:14

The Barrage

Here comes a barrage of pent-up tears, frustration, anger—seemingly from nowhere. I both expect it and don't expect it. I can see it coming but I never know where it comes from.

What can I do about it?

Nothing.

I am powerless before your resentments.

We are powerless against this great multitude that is coming against us. We do not know what to do, but our eyes are upon you.

2 Chronicles 20:12

The Unthinkable—Part 2

Their marriage survived the unthinkable—the accidental death of one of their children. We don't understand how they were able to accept the tragedy without somehow blaming each other. Many marriages run aground on such sharp, painful shoals.

It wasn't easy—they both will tell you that. They even separated for a while. But somehow they found their way back to each other.

Lord, may our marriage never be put to such a test.

"And do not bring us to the time of trial."
Luke 11:4

Sacred Memories

You hold so many memories for me. Memories of all we have shared—the good times and the bad.

You hold them within you. They are there when we touch, when we make love. They are sacred to me.

No one else holds memories for me like you do.

I thank my God every time I remember you.
                                        Philippians 1:3

Detachment

The opposite of love isn't hate; it's detachment.

To be detached is to take something and place it under a microscope to be analyzed and observed. Relationships are not meant to be analyzed; they are meant to be lived.

Do we have the courage to eschew detachment and take our chances with love?

———————————————

"I know your works, you are neither cold nor hot. I wish that you were either cold or hot. So, because you are lukewarm, and neither cold nor hot, I am about to spit you out of my mouth."

Revelation 3:15-16

| A Mystery—Part 3 |

No matter how we try to get to the bottom of things, the heart of marriage remains a mystery to be lived.

Beloved, let us love one another, because love is from God; everyone who loves is born of God and knows God....Beloved, since God loved us so much, we also ought to love one another.

1 John 4:7, 11

> ### Reconnecting

Sometimes it only takes a moment to reconnect:

a caress

a peck on the cheek

a hug

a whispered nothing

a look.

---

*The wise remain silent until the right
moment, but a boasting fool misses the
right moment.*

Sirach 20:7

Will He Notice?

I was the one who used to "work" at the relationship. Preparing candlelight dinners, arranging romantic evenings out. But after so many years, I'm tired of doing it.

Why does it always have to be me who takes the first step, makes all the arrangements? Why can't he put in some effort too?

I'm tired. I'm not going to do it anymore.

Will he even notice?

"Where did you glean today? And where did you work? Blessed be the man who took notice of you."

Ruth 2:19

He Noticed

One day I realized that she had stopped arranging candlelight dinners and evenings out. Funny, at first I was relieved. No more pressure to get dressed up. I could sit in front of the TV as much as I liked.

But it's starting to bug me.

What's going on here? Something's not quite right.

Should I be the first to break the silence?

Then she fell prostrate, with her face to the ground, and said to him, "Why have I found favor in your sight, that you should take notice of me?"

Ruth 2:10

We Are and We Aren't

Sometimes I wish we weren't so much of who we are and that we were more of who we aren't.

―――――――――

Now to him who by the power at work
within us is able to accomplish abundantly
far more than all we can ask or imagine, to
him be glory in the church and in Christ
Jesus to all generations, forever and ever.
Amen.

Ephesians 3:20-21

Trust—Part 2

Do you trust me enough to see through me, into what lies in my heart?

Do I trust you enough to believe you'll tell me if there is something wrong between us?

Let me hear of your steadfast love in the morning, for in you I put my trust. Teach me the way I should go, for to you I lift up my soul.

Psalm 143:8

> *Enough Love—Part 1*

She gets excited about the kids and their friends. "Aren't they cute?" she says.

After a while, he slinks off into his workroom to put in a few hours. She shows up at the door.

"I thought after the kids go to bed we might, you know, fool around."

His heart jumps.

"I've got some more work to do."

"When you're done."

"When I'm done."

He smiles.

"What are you smiling at?"

"You. I'm smiling at you."

He realizes once again that there is always enough love to go around.

The righteous have enough to satisfy their appetite, but the belly of the wicked is empty.

Proverbs 13:25

"In a Zone"

It used to happen for him in high school.

On the basketball court, he could "see" what was going to happen before it did happen. He was "in a zone", "going with the flow." He couldn't miss. It was so easy.

As his playing days wound down, he thought he would never again experience this feeling.

Then he met her. He's been "in a zone" ever since.

In that day the mountains shall drip sweet wine, the hills shall flow with milk, and all the stream beds of Judah shall flow with water.

Joel 3:18

Easy

Being married to him is easy for her. He always respects her opinions, her interests, her abilities, her contributions to their family.

She admires him for his physical and spiritual strength, for his passions, for his commitment and sensitivity to others.

She is still infatuated with his looks, his personality, his intelligence, his integrity.

Who wouldn't want to be married to this guy?

One man among a thousand I found.
Ecclesiastes 7:28

Still Crazy

There's that certain look he gets and I know he's up to something. A certain smile, a curl of impish delight. I may not know exactly what he's about to do, but he's up to something. I groan inwardly and try to brace myself for whatever will happen next. He sneaks up on me from behind, pounces like a lion on his prey, and says "Gotcha." I break into a thousand giggles.

There's that certain look she gets: quiet, pensive. I know she's worried about something, whether it's the bills, the kids, or her parents' health. It's written all over her face. I sneak up on her, snap on the music, and say "Gotcha." She laughs despite herself.

All were amazed and perplexed, saying to one another, "What does this mean?" But others sneered and said, "They are filled with new wine."

Acts 2:12-13

Thought Waves

I will never understand how her brain works. She pulls conclusions out of the air, seemingly from nowhere. There is no logical pattern to her thought process. She jumps from one thought to another, making incredible mental leaps. And yet she can be surprisingly creative...and even right!

I'll never understand him. He is so damn logical. C follows B which follows A. The quickest way to get from one point to another is a straight line—and for him it's the only way. Not me! I like to detour down unexplored avenues, cruise alleyways and dead-end streets until, suddenly, connection happens.

Women! There's no reasoning with them

Men! They're so predictable.

I pray that you may have the power to comprehend, with all the saints, what is the breadth and length and height and depth, and to know the love of Christ that sur-passes knowledge, so that you may be filled with all the fullness of God.

Ephesians 3:18-19

Appreciation—Part 3

Sometimes you have to be alone

to appreciate what you have together.

(I cried out,) "I will praise your name
continually, and will sing hymns of thanks-
giving." My prayer was heard, for you
saved me from destruction and rescued me
in time of trouble. For this reason I thank
you and praise you, and I bless the name of
the Lord.

Sirach 51:11-12

| *Cold Mornings* |

Mornings when the temperature drops I draw you close and hold you tight for warmth.

Thank you, God, for cold mornings, when the frost comes and we cuddle for warmth.

If two lie together, they keep warm; but how can one keep warm alone?
> *Ecclesiastes 4:11*

Mind Reading—Part 2

She hears his voice even now. Through the infinite distance, across a vale of tears, he still speaks to her.

Even though he is gone, he is still with her, in her mind and in her heart.

The voice of my beloved! Look, he comes, leaping upon the mountains, bounding over the hills. My beloved is like a gazelle or a young stag. Look, there he stands behind our wall, gazing in at the windows, looking through the lattice.
Song of Songs 2:8-9

> *Because of You*

You bring out the best in me.

You bring out parts of me I didn't even realize existed.

I am a very different person because of you.

I am a very different person because of you.

It is harmful to drink wine alone, or, again, to drink water alone, while wine mixed with water is sweet and delicious and enhances one's enjoyment.

2 Maccabees 15:39

| Keep Trying—Part 2 |

When it comes to love,

we never completely learn.

We just keep trying.

Rejoice in hope, be patient in suffering,
persevere in prayer.

Romans 12:12

Not This Time

"What?" she says from the doorway.

"What?" he answers.

"What are you thinking?" she asks.

He looks at her.

"You have that look on your face," she says.

"So?" he answers. "Does it have to mean something?"

"It usually does," she says.

But he doesn't unmask himself. It takes too much energy and he has had a long day.

"Not this time," he says.

(There is) a time to tear, and a time to sew;
a time to keep silence, and a time to speak.
                                    Ecclesiastes 3:7

Advice Giving / Taking

At first—or at least early on in their relationship—he used to feel that every time she asked his
advice he had to have an answer. He was flattered that
she would seek his input, but after a while he noticed
that she didn't always do what he suggested. That put
him out.

"Why ask me if you don't take my advice?" he
complained.

But she kept on asking, and he kept on answering. She trusted his advice, but she wanted to make up
her own mind.

But take care and watch yourself closely,
so as neither to forget the things that your
eyes have seen nor to let them slip from
your mind all the days of your life.
Deuteronomy 4:9

An Equal

He can still feel like a little boy who needs mothering, a spoiled child who needs to be reminded that there are other people in the world, a thwarted athlete who needs encouragement, a frustrated student who needs to be nurtured.

So sometimes he looks to his wife to be, in turn, a mother, a disciplinarian, a coach, a mentor.

But he has learned that what he really needs is an equal who reminds him that he is who he is, and that she loves him for that.

Just as woman came from man, so man comes through woman; but all things come from God.

1 Corinthians 11:12

Vacation

They unexpectedly got away for a week. It was an opportunity they couldn't pass up. For the first time in ages, no one called from work, no children interrupted their vacation. He golfed. She shopped. They ate wonderful meals, lay in the sun, made love.

"I didn't think it would ever be like this again," he confessed.

"I wish it could last forever," she confided.

Bless the LORD, O my soul, and do not forget all his benefits—who forgives all your iniquity, who heals all your diseases, who redeems your life from the Pit, who crowns you with steadfast love and mercy, who satisfies you with good as long as you live so that your youth is renewed like the eagle's.

Psalm 103:2-4

The Fight

I hate it when she cowers like that.

I hate it when he yells so.

It makes me feel like an ogre.

It makes me feel so small and alone.

I'm not going to hurt her.

I know he's not going to hurt me.

So why does she cower?

But why does he have to yell so?

---

*Remember, O Lord; make yourself known
in this time of affliction, and give me
courage, O King of the gods and Master of
all dominion! Put eloquent speech in my
mouth before the lion, and turn his heart to
hate the man who is fighting against us, so
that there may be an end to him.*
Esther 14:12-13

The Future

After so many years of marriage, we probably don't know any more about what the future holds than on the day we wed.

What's different is that now we know that we're a team and that we'll face the future—whatever it holds—together.

We are God's servants, working together.
1 Corinthians 3:9

> ### Don't Hurry

Don't hurry. Be happy.

You must understand this, my beloved: let everyone be quick to listen, slow to speak, slow to anger; for your anger does not produce God's righteousness.

James 1:19-20

The Promise

"Hi, Mom, we're home. Surprise!" The children run in excitedly holding a small brown puppy. Her husband brings up the rear and grins sheepishly.

"We'll take care of her, Mom, don't worry," they all promise.

"I'm sure you will," she says. "We'll talk about this later," her eyes add to her husband.

"Sure they'll take care of you," she says to the puppy the next day. "Sure they will."

"Well, come on," she sighs, and together they watch her favorite soap. She scratches the puppy's ears and cuddles it.

---

*I rise before dawn and cry for help; I put
my hope in your words. My eyes are awake
before each watch of the night, that I may
meditate on your promise.*
Psalm 119:147-148

A Couple's Prayer

God, help us remember that—in addition to all the effort we put into our relationship—you are there, still working to make sure things come out in accordance with your will.

———————————————

Rejoice always, pray without ceasing, give thanks in all circumstances; for this is the will of God in Christ Jesus for you.
1 Thessalonians 5:16-18

> New Territory

When the phone call came that her favorite niece had died, he grew very silent, because this really wasn't his territory. He put an arm around her shoulders so that she could cry into his chest. His own tears, unnoticed, fell freely and landed on her hair.

_____

"Blessed are those who mourn, for they will be comforted."

Matthew 5:4

> *Taken for Granted*

How quickly

we take for granted

what we have,

unless and until

we are threatened

with losing it.

Those who try to make their lives secure
will lose it, but those who lose their life will
keep it. I tell you, on that night there will be
two in one bed; one will be taken and the
other left.

Luke 17:33-34

> ### What Women Want

The secret of what a woman wants, King Arthur discovered, is to be what she wants to be when she wants to be it.

Knowing that secret saved Arthur's neck.

It could save every husband's at some point in his marriage.

_____

A desire realized is sweet to the soul.
                    Proverbs 13:19

What Men Want

Every man wants to be made to feel important by a woman, preferably his wife.

Women who accomplish that one task have no problems with the rest.

Oh yeah, let them watch a game once in a while too.

A woman's beauty lights up a man's face, and there is nothing he desires more. If kindness and humility mark her speech, her husband is more fortunate than other men.
                    Sirach 36:27-28

Remarriage

He brought his brokenness into their relationship. She brought hers. They couldn't be everything for each other, but they were enough. They helped each other heal and become whole.

———————————————

At that very moment, the prayers of both of them were heard in the glorious presence of God. So Raphael was sent to heal them both.

Tobit 3:16-17

Hierarchy

Why does there have to be a hierarchy of love?
Can't we love everyone equally, but treat them differently based on differing needs? Why do we have an
obsession with assigning rank?

I love you. You are important to me. Isn't that
enough?

---

*One of the scribes came near and heard
them disputing with one another, and
seeing that he answered them well, he
asked him, "Which commandment is the
first of all?" Jesus answered, "The first is,
'Hear, O Israel: the Lord our God, the
Lord is one; you shall love the Lord your
God with all your heart, and with all your
soul, and with all your mind, and with all
your strength.' The second is this, 'You
shall love your neighbor as yourself.' There
is no other commandment greater than
these."*

Mark 12:28-31

The Spice of Life

Some people like to try endless variety, always sampling something new, flitting from one thing to the next, never satisfied.

They say variety is the spice of life. Not so for me. Let me feast on a daily diet of you.

How sweet is your love, my sister, my bride! how much better is your love than wine, and the fragrance of your oils than any spice!

Song of Songs 4:10

Porcupine Love

Q: How do porcupines make love?

A: Very carefully.

Q: How do humans make love?

A: Very carefully.

Then (God) said: "Come no closer!
Remove the sandals from your feet, for the
place on which you are standing is holy
ground."

Exodus 3:5

Love Story—Part 2

It seems that in Hollywood a good love story has to involve extraordinary events, great excitement, explosive passion, and often a tragic ending.

I'd like our love story to be a relatively boring one about two people who meet, come together, marry, and forge a solid, faithful (and faith-filled) relationship through daily encounters with each other in a busy but stimulating environment.

Then, we live happily ever after!

The LORD bless you from Zion. May you see the prosperity of Jerusalem all the days of your life. May you see your children's children. Peace be upon Israel!
                                        Psalm 128:5-6

Please tell me what you want, when you want it.

_____

You covet something and cannot obtain it;
so you engage in disputes and conflicts.
You do not have, because you do not ask.
                                        James 4:2

Alone

Marriage isn't an escape from aloneness. It is an entering into the great mystery of aloneness with another person.

There is one body and one Spirit, just as you were called to the one hope of your calling, one Lord, one faith, one baptism, one God and Father of all, who is above all and through all and in all.

Ephesians 4:4-5

Unwelcome Guest

Cancer has come to call—an uninvited, unwelcome guest who refuses to leave. Alien, invisible, it has taken up residence in his spouse's body.

But it is killing both of them.

"Where you die, I will die—there will I be buried. May the LORD do thus and so to me, and more as well, if even death parts me from you."

Ruth 1:17

Grateful

There are so many things I am grateful for in my life: our health, our home, our children, the memories we share. But more than anything, I am thankful for the gift of your friendship throughout these many years.

I know I may show it in strange ways. I'm not all that good with words. I'm clumsy about sentimental things, but that doesn't change how I feel. Even if I don't say it, I am grateful for your presence in my life.

What do you have that you did not receive? And if you received it, why do you boast as if it were not a gift? Already you have all you want! Already you have become rich!
1 Corinthians 4:7-8

Little / Big Things

She gave in to him on all the little decisions—like what TV shows to watch or when to eat—and thereby she kept the peace in their marriage.

It was only on the big questions that she stood her ground, refusing to budge.

Perhaps it would have been better to fight over the little things and be willing to compromise on the big ones.

———————————————

Too long have I had my dwelling among those who hate peace. I am for peace; but when I speak, they are for war.

Psalm 120:6-7

Viva la Différence

I watch my wife with our daughter. There's a special bond they have—female to female—that I'll never have with either one of them

I watch my husband with our son. Boys will be boys, and men will be men—and I'll never be either.

She is introducing our daughter into a world of women I can only observe as an outsider.

He is training our son in the ways of men, ways I can appreciate but never fully comprehend

———————————

When God created humankind, he made them in the likeness of God. Male and female he created them, and named them "Humankind" when they were created.
Genesis 5:1-2

Two Couples

Both couples fight, but there the resemblance ends.

Underlying the one couple's spats is a loving, playful give and take, almost like two lion cubs batting each other around in play.

Underneath the other couple's battles are indifference, hatred, a persistent unhappiness like a nagging toothache that never goes away.

Well meant are the wounds a friend inflicts,
but profuse are the kisses of an enemy.
                                        Proverbs 27:6

Looking Back—Part 2

We are told not to look over our shoulders because something bad may be gaining on us. But that's just silly.

We must look backward if we are to remember where we have come from. Only then will we find the reasons for pushing forward.

The key to looking back productively is to do so with the expectation and intention of finding the good things—things we suspected were there all along but we weren't exactly able to put our fingers on.

(God) has made everything suitable for its time; moreover he has put a sense of past and future into their minds.

Ecclesiastes 3:11

| *Getting Help* |

There are unconscious forces at work within all married couples, pulling us apart. They bring out the worst in each of us as we both play out scenarios from our childhoods.

Those scenarios will win. The past will continue to repeat itself. The unconscious will continue to play and replay, controlling our lives...unless we stop, learn from our past, break the cycle, get the help we need.

For I do not do the good I want, but the evil I do not want is what I do.

Romans 7:19

Enough Love—Part 2

God, help us to remember that you will ensure that there is always enough love to go around, especially when it comes to married couples.

I am confident of this, that the one who began a good work among you will bring it to completion by the day of Jesus Christ....And this is my prayer, that your love may overflow more and more with knowledge and full insight to help you to determine what is best, so that in the day of Christ you may be pure and blameless, having produced the harvest of righteousness that comes through Jesus Christ for the glory and praise of God.
Philippians 1:6, 9-11

Advent

Being a busy couple is fine—we get things done quickly, efficiently and on time. We wouldn't want it any other way.

But the season of Advent reminds us of the value of waiting for something. The anticipation, the you-can't-have-it-yet feeling, forces us to think about what can still be, what we can still become.

Let us take this time to anticipate the rest of our lives together. Let the waiting fill us with good tidings.

"Nothing will be impossible with God."
Luke 1:37

Waiting

I've had plenty of experience waiting! Waiting for you to get dressed. Waiting for you to finish the project you started last year. Waiting for you to decide you're ready to talk about making a decision. Waiting for you to be ready to make a decision.

For all my practice, it doesn't get any easier.

_____

Wait for the LORD; be strong, and let your heart take courage; wait for the LORD!
                                             Psalm 27:14

Shared Faith

He goes to his church. She goes to hers. Sometimes they go together to each other's church.

They almost broke up about it before they got married, but they thought they had worked out a solution to allow each other their individual expression of faith. Still, now and then the issue comes up again. It is one of the greatest challenges of their married life.

Like all challenges, it can split them apart...or their lives can be enriched by the two faiths they share.

As many of you as were baptized into Christ have clothed yourselves with Christ....If you belong to Christ, then you are Abraham's offspring, heirs according to the promise.

Galatians 3:27, 29

Don't

When I tell you I hurt,
     don't make it all better.

When I tell you I'm lonely,
     don't save me from the feeling.

When I tell you I'm afraid,
     don't protect me.

When I tell you I'm jealous,
     don't judge me.

When I tell you I'm angry,
     don't condemn me.

Don't analyze me,
     rescue me,
     save me from myself,
     or control me.

---

*If you accept my words and treasure up
my commandments within you, making
your ear attentive to wisdom and inclining
your heart to understanding; if you indeed
cry out for insight and raise your voice for
understanding; if you seek it like silver,
and search for it as for hidden treasures—
then you will understand.*

                          Proverbs 2:1-5

No One Knows

No one else knows what goes on between a couple. We sometimes wonder why some people stay together when they seem so unhappy, while others who seem so happy end up separated.

The inner workings of a human being are marvelously complex. How two human beings come together to form a marriage is even more intricate. What works for some couples, doesn't work for others. What may be a saving grace in one marriage, may be the downfall of another.

No one knows what goes on between a couple, except the couple themselves...and even they are in the dark most of the time.

"You will indeed listen, but never understand, and you will indeed look, but never perceive."

Matthew 13:14

The Affair

She watches as the young couple proclaim their love forever. Memories of that terrible day when she found out about her husband's affair flood her mind. How incredibly that hurt. She didn't know if she could ever trust him again. Her friends had told her to leave him; infidelity was surely grounds for divorce. But for some reason she had stayed. The two of them worked it out. God gave her the grace to forgive. She was glad she did.

He, too, recalled the years of their marriage as he watched the ceremony. "Young man," he thought, "don't do what I did. Don't be led astray to make the same mistake. I'll never forget the look on my wife's face when she found out about my affair. The hurt I caused her. She's forgiven me, but I've yet to forgive myself. I have to live with the memory of how much I hurt this woman I love."

All this is from God, who reconciled us to himself through Christ, and has given us the ministry of reconciliation; that is, in Christ God was reconciling the world to himself, not counting their trespasses against them, and entrusting the message of reconciliation to us.

2 Corinthians 5:18-19

> *One Thing at a Time*

"Don't worry," he tells her. "We'll take one thing at a time."

That is the way she likes it.

He likes it that way too. Taking one thing at a time, one day at a time, one decision at a time. Sounds so easy, but they both know it is a gift. And they are mighty grateful for it.

"So do not worry about tomorrow, for tomorrow will bring worries of its own. Today's trouble is enough for today."
                              Matthew 6:34

| Communication |

God, somehow—through all the craziness—
we've got to keep the lines of communication open.
Help us to be flexible and use whatever means are
available—notes on napkins, telephone messages,
roses, special friendship cards, a look here, the squeeze
of a hand there.

"I have a message from God for you."
Judges 3:20

┌─────────────────┐
│ *"Us"—Part 1* │
└─────────────────┘

It used to be that I was the one who wanted to talk about "us"—to know where we stood with each other. He always resisted such conversation. So we learned to talk around it. We talk about everything else but "us," and it's okay. I've gotten used to it. I'm comfortable.

But now he wants to talk about "us." After so many years of marriage, why this sudden change? Long ago, I would have been ecstatic. Now I'm the one who's uncomfortable.

Have windy words no limit? Or what provokes you that you keep on talking? I also could talk as you do, if you were in my place.

Job 16:3-4

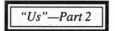

She always used to want to talk about "us." She wanted to share "intimate feelings." I wanted nothing to do with it. Wasn't it enough that I married her? Didn't that say how I felt?

But I've changed. There's this nagging emptiness inside. It's hard to describe. I want to share my hopes and dreams and disappointments with her. After all this time I thought she'd be happy that I want to talk, but she isn't. Now she's threatened.

Well, if anyone should be able to understand that feeling, I should.

I could encourage you with my mouth, and the solace of my lips would assuage your pain.

Job 16:5

Money—Part 2

No matter how much money I make, it's never enough. We always have to pinch and save. I never feel like I can spend money on myself or go out with the guys. She holds the purse strings, and I'm being strangled.

I offered to let him take over our finances. I'm willing to give this chore up. It's not like I enjoy being the one who decides how we spend our money. He never understands where the money goes. If he paid the bills for a month, he'd start to see things differently. Just give me an allowance and let him worry about the rest.

I hate having to ask permission.

I hate being the miser.

Hear but a little of my instruction, and through me you will acquire silver and gold. May your soul rejoice in God's mercy, and may you never be ashamed to praise him. Do your work in good time, and in his own time God will give you your reward.

Sirach 51:28-30

Chores

If I talk about chores and equal division of labor he balks. "That's not love. Love's not fifty-fifty, tit for tat," he says. How can I argue with that?

"We should do work around the home because we want to," she tells me. "We should just do it without worrying who did what, when." How can I argue with that?

Then why do I feel like I'm getting the short end of the stick?

Then why do I feel I'm doing more than my fair share?

Then they said to him, "What must we do to perform the works of God?" Jesus answered them, "This is the work of God, that you believe in him whom he has sent."
                                        John 6:28-29

I surprise her with cards and flowers now and then. I even do the dishes and vacuum the rugs. That's more than most of the men I know do. And I do it because I want to. Still, she isn't happy. What more does she want?

I appreciate his little gifts and I know he does more around the house than most men. Why can't I just appreciate what I have and be happy? What else do I want?

To whom will you liken me and make me equal, and compare me, as though we were alike?

Isaiah 46:5

Going Out

"Going out again?" she asks.

"Yes, I've got that meeting at church."

I resent all the time he spends at church. It seems that every spare minute goes there, but how can I say anything? After all, it's not like he's going out drinking with the guys. Those other people need him. Isn't it wrong to resent time given to God?

"Going out again?" he asks.

"Yes, PTA meeting."

I resent all the time she spends with civic activities—PTA, Boy Scouts, Girl Scouts. But how can I complain? She's doing it for the kids, isn't she? I shouldn't resent my own kids.

"Going out again?" they both ask.

Yes, but not together.

Only acknowledge your guilt, that you have rebelled against the Lord your God, and scattered your favors among strangers under every green tree.

Jeremiah 3:13

> *Surprise Me*

What should we do today?

Surprise me!

_____

*"Be dressed for action and have your
lamps lit."*

Matthew 12:35

Fun

Fun is getting away for a night and going to a first-run movie or a cheap movie house to see a movie that all our friends have raved about.

Fun is using the gift certificate from your birthday in March so that we can go out to dinner in June.

Fun is slipping away together for a shopping trip that you would ordinarily take on your own.

Fun is meeting you after work at a place where we can talk uninterrupted.

Fun is dropping by an old friend's house where we watch reruns of *Home Improvement* or *Murphy Brown*.

Rejoice in the Lord always; again I say rejoice.

Philippians 4:4

$$\boxed{\textit{Together / Apart}}$$

Together, yet apart—even in our most intimate moments.

For moments we are one, then we are again two.

Still, something remains that is more than the two of us individually. And that something grows greater with time.

"They are no longer two, but one."
Matthew 19:6

White Light

He calls it the white light of love. She is this light. There are times it surrounds him, warm and inviting, open and welcoming.

Sometimes it is simply too much though. It overwhelms him. He wants to scream.

That can be scary. He is afraid he will lose himself in her.

Because you have made the LORD your refuge, the Most High your dwelling place, no evil shall befall you, no scourge come near your tent. For he will command his angels concerning you to guard you in all your ways. On their hands they will bear you up, so that you will not dash your foot against a stone.

Psalm 91:9-12

Our Time

God, help us make the most of our time together, for we know neither the day nor the hour.

For you yourselves know very well that the day of the Lord will come as a thief in the night. When they say, "There is peace and security," then sudden destruction will come upon them, as labor pains come upon a pregnant woman, and there will be no escape! But you, beloved, are not in darkness, for that day to surprise you like a thief; for you are all children of light and children of the day; we are not of darkness.
1 Thessalonians 5:2-5

Party Time!

What *isn't* there to celebrate?

Our relationship?

Our separate accomplishments?

Our family?

Our growth as individuals and as a couple?

Let's face it: It's party time!

---

*Now at the dedication of the wall of
Jerusalem they sought out the Levites in all
their places, to bring them to Jerusalem to
celebrate the dedication with rejoicing,
with thanksgivings and with singing, with
cymbals, harps, and lyres.*

Nehemiah 12:27

> *Celebrating*

What is it that we are celebrating this time of year, anyway? A child was born to a young girl and her adoring husband.

On the surface, it wasn't such a big deal. It happens all the time.

What makes it memorable is the risk that the couple took to respond to something that they could not comprehend, could not control, and could not afford.

Like we said, it happens all the time!

When Joseph awoke from sleep, he did as the angel of the Lord commanded him; he took (Mary) as his wife.

Matthew 1:24

Q: When does one half plus one half not equal one whole?

A: When it's a marriage. You need two whole people to form one whole marriage.

Their descendents shall be known among the nations, and their offspring among the peoples; all who see them shall acknowledge that they are people whom the LORD has blessed.

Isaiah 61:9

Hints and Signs

The stuff of Christmas is full of the hints of God—the decorated tree, the candles on the table, the presents we give others and others give us.

And we, a couple in the midst of all this busy activity, are ourselves signs of God's goodness to each other and for the world to see.

The signs of a true apostle were performed among you with utmost patience, signs and wonders and mighty works.
2 Corinthians 12:12

Light of the World

If it is better to light one little candle than to curse the darkness, how much better if we light two!

_____

"Let your light shine before others, so that
they may see your good works and give
glory to your Father in heaven."
                                    Matthew 5:16

Christmas is about the incarnation of the divine in human flesh.

Who better symbolizes that miracle than a loving married couple?

———————————————————

The Word became flesh and lived among us.

John 1:14

Flesh

How good is the flesh,

soft the skin,

pleasant the hair,

firm the bones.

How good it is

to know you

in the biblical sense.

---

*I will greatly rejoice in the LORD, my whole
being shall exult in my God; for he has
clothed me with the garments of salvation, he
has covered me with the robe of righteousness, as a bridegroom decks himself with a
garland, and as a bride adorns herself with
her jewels.*

Isaiah 61:10

The Price

Everything worthwhile comes with a price tag. The greater the cost, the more it is valued.

Our marriage has cost me the best part of my life.

And so I value it beyond measure.

Truly, no ransom avails for one's life, there is no price one can give to God for it. For the ransom of life is costly, and can never suffice.

Psalm 49:7-8

A Couple—Part 2

Slowly, they take down the ornaments and decorations from Christmas one by one. After so many years, they are a great team: assigning each other tasks, anticipating each other's needs, sharing inside jokes, recalling fond memories.

They are a couple.

As God's chosen ones, holy and beloved, clothe yourselves with compassion, kindness, humility, meekness, and patience. Bear with one another and, if anyone has a complaint against another, forgive each other; just as the Lord has forgiven you, so you also must forgive. Above all, clothe yourselves with love, which binds everything together in perfect harmony.
Colossians 3:12-14

"For better or for worse; in sickness and in health; until death do us part...."

When we made our wedding vows we knew neither what we were promising nor whether we could keep them.

We know both answers a little better now, because we have lived those vows.

Thank you for being my spouse, my lover, my friend—for better *and* for worse.

Many proclaim themselves loyal, but who can find one worthy of trust?

Proverbs 20:6

As another year with you

comes to an end,

I await new beginnings

that make for new beginnings...

that make for new beginnings....

The beginnings are manifest in wonders.
                    2 Esdras 9:6

I Love You

I may not always say it, but I love you.

I know you do, and I love you too

That is all we ever need.

———————————

My God will fully satisfy every need of yours according to his riches in glory in Christ Jesus.

> *Philippians 4:19*